Professional Stage Hypnotism

FOR ORDER OR CATALOG
WESTWOOD PUBLISHING COMPANY
700 S. Central Avenue
Glendale, CA 91204

Published by Westwood Publishing Company
Glendale, CA 91204

ISBN 0-930298-03-9

Printed in the United States of America

Contents

Preface

My first introduction to Stage Hypnotism occured when I was twelve years old. My mother's cousin (known to me as "Uncle David") came to visit us and after dinner he amazed everyone with his sleight of hand and other magic tricks. I was not overly impressed with magic tricks, but then "Uncle Dave" stated that he would hypnotize anyone who wished it.

I was hesitant, but both my father and mother were quickly put into a trance and I watched with awe as they followed his every command. Imagine the significance of seeing my authority figures seemingly surrender their personal authority to someone else.

This so excited my imagination that for the next several years, I tried to learn more about this mysterious power. Unfortunely, I was not able to find any books in the library (1937-1938), only a brief explanation in the encyclopedia.

My enthusiasm for hypnotism remained constant as did my ignorance of the subject.

Then in 1947, I discovered a book that changed my life. It was called THE ENCYCLOPEDIA OF STAGE HYPNOTISM by Ormond McGill. For the first time I had instruction, clearly set down with an assurance I could easily hypnotize **ANYONE.**

As the years passed and my devotion to hypnotism created a career for me, I came to know Ormond McGill and to call him friend.

Today thirty-one years later, I am thrilled and delighted to have the special honor of publishing "Professional Stage Hypnotism". This is a totally revised and updated version of the "Encyclopedia of Stage Hypnotism" that was such an important influence in my life.

It is with pride and appreciation, I present to you, Ormond McGill and "Professional Stage Hypnotism".

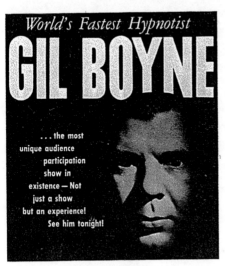

World's Fastest Hypnotist

GIL BOYNE

... the most unique audience participation show in existence — Not just a show but an experience! See him tonight!

Theatrical Poster
used by Gil Boyne 1959

Gil Boyne — President
Westwood Publishing Co.

AUTHORS
Introduction

Stage hypotism provides absolutely fascinating entertainment. It combines the sensational with human interest producing a program that is amazing, amusing, and thought-provoking.

Part one of this book teaches you the science of hypnotism, and shows you how to expertly hynotize. Part two instructs in how to perform stage hypnotism to make it fine entertainment that everyone will appreciate. It lifts demonstrations in hynotism to the status of an art, and takes great care to give directions for the careful handling of hypnotic effects which will always produce the most pleasant experiences to be enjoyed by both those volunteering as subjects in the experiments as well as the spectators[1]. As quality entertainment, professional stage hynotism emphasizes the important and valuable work being performed in medical and academic fields in relation to hypnosis.

No form of entertaining is more basically appealing than the hypnotic exhibition. It is one of the very few types of shows which may be seen over and over and never lose its fascination, as every program is different. People like people, and as the hypnotism show is devoted entirely to audience participation entertainment one never knows what surprises are going to happen. There is something so warmly human, while, at the same time, verging on the mysterious, that hypnotism stands unique in the entertainment field. Normally staid audiences have been literally convulsed with laughter in watching the fun-filled antics of hypnotic subjects upon the stage; a few minutes later, that same audience has leaned forward in their seats staring in wonder at the phenomena unfolding before their eyes.

It is natural that this is so, as the human mind is the greatest wonder and mystery of all. *Hypnotism demonstrates the magic-of-the-mind.*

Within these pages will be found not only step-by-step instructions in hypnotism and how to become an expert hypnotic entertainer presenting a remarkable program for parties, social gatherings, lectures, and stage demonstrations, but the performing subtleties, insights, and details of hypnotic presentation, that come only from experience, are included making this one of the most valuable books of its kind ever offered. Also, the nonperformer will find a wealth of knowledge about the psychology of hypnotism and its practical application, as stage hypnotism provides the means of acquainting thousands of people with this wonder science of the ages.

Both text and diagrammatic illustrations educe an education in the art of stage hypnotism, and functions as a textbook dealing with this popular phase of hypnotic phenomena in filling a niche in the growing literature related to the various aspects of hypnosis.

1. *Hynotism must never be regarded as a toy that you play with to entertain yourself. The human mind is a delicate instrument which must be handled with great care and respect. Remember, the hynotist has a legal and moral obligation to approach the performance of hypnotism in a completely ethical manner, and appreciate that the most important person in his presentation is the subject and not himself.*

PART ONE:

THE ART OF HYPNOTIZING

1
Obtaining Your
First Subjects

Professional Stage Hypnotism takes you from the very beginning of learning how to hypnotize to the culmination of staging a complete hypnotism show. This handling will instruct you thoroughly as you must first learn the psychological skill of inducing hypnosis before you can successfully entertain with the science/art.

The ability to hypnotize flawlessly comes with practice, and for that purpose your very first objective is to secure subjects who are interested in your work, and who wish to experiment with hypnosis. Through such practice you will become a master of the technique.

From experience, it will be found that most people prefer to approach the matter of being hypnotized in a gradual manner. If you suggest immediately that they submit to being fully hypnotized (entering the hypnotic trance) some will shy away from it, but a little diplomacy in first attempting lighter hypnotic phenomena goes a long way in building confidence to try for more advanced experimenting later on. Further, this is correct training,as at this initial stage very possibly you might not be able to induce complete hypnosis, while you may readily demonstrate lighter forms of phenomena.

In hypnotizing, it is important to build the subject's confidence in the matter of being hypnotized just as it is important to build your own confidence as a hypnotist. I have always looked upon the induction of hypnosis as a dynamic situation. Success begets success, and it is highly desirable that you achieve positive results right from the start. Possibly there is no more important rule in the whole art of hypnotizing than this one:

To be a successful hypnotist you must have confidence in your ability to hypnotize, and nothing builds confidence like successful hypnotizing.

These preliminary tests, which you will now learn how to perform, are important to your success as a hypnotist as your subject will find himself (or herself) responding -- step by step -- to your experiments, as you gradually advance him up-the-ladder towards achieving complete hypnosis. Use this approach:

Find some congenial person who has an intelligent interest in psychology, and direct the conversation toward the proven fact that many people find it difficult to relax completely. Then propose a little test in relaxation.

Note that no mention of hypnotism has been made up to this point, and this very first experiment arouses interest and leads naturally into advancing experiments. Also, it is a test you can perform effectively with one person or with a group.

Explain that the ability to obtain complete mental and physical rest comes in direct proportion to the ability to relax, and that many people think they know how to relax while actually they are tense the majority of the time.

To illustrate the point, have the person (or persons, as the case may be) raise his left arm up at a right angle in front of his chest, then extend the forefinger of his right hand and place it directly under the palm of his left hand. In such a position, the extended finger is ready to support the entire weight of the left hand and arm. See Fig. 1.

Now tell him to completely relax his left hand and arm, the extended finger of his right hand being the sole support of his arm. He is thus placed in a situation that requires the relaxing of the left arm while, at the same time, concentrating on holding it up with the extended finger of the right hand. You have here a situation requiring simultaneously both concentration and relaxation – a condition very similar to that required for the induction of hypnotists.

Next, the party being confident that his left hand and arm are entirely relaxed, you instruct him further, "At the count of three, you are to quickly draw your forefinger from beneath the relaxed hand, and drop it to your lap."

You then count slowly, "One, two, three . . .What happens? If the subject has followed your instructions and performed the experiment correctly, the moment he withdraws the support from under his left hand, that arm naturally drops limply to his lap. Such is the obvious result if the arm is really relaxed, as shown in Fig. 2.

Fig. 1

Fig. 2

But, as frequently proves the case, in many instances the subject's left arm will not drop but will remain still suspended in the air even after the finger support is withdrawn. When this occurs, it indicates, of course, that the person was not really relaxed as he thought himself to be. See Fig. 3.

Explain the situation to the subject, emphasizing the truth that often people think they are relaxed when in reality they remain tense, as is indicated by his so-called relaxed arm failing to fall to his lap. Have him then repeat the experiment, being sure to himself that this time his left hand and arm are truly relaxed. Again you count, "One, two, three," and he withdraws the finger support, and accordingly he is almost certain now to have obtained the desired condition, relaxation, as his left hand drops limply into his lap.

Having completed this first test in relaxation successfully, explain to your experimenting subject that another interesting curiosity of the mind to consider is the fact that when an idea of action is concentrated upon, it will realize itself in unconscious movements. Psychologist, William James termed this effect, "ideo-motor action."

You are now ready to try some further experimenting.

Fig. 3

2
Preliminary Tests
With Suggestion

The experiments you will now introduce to your potential subject(s) are known as "posture sway demonstrations."

As a test, ask your subject to stand erect with his feet together. Explain to him that in this experiment you will show how unconscious muscular actions will develop in direct response to thought, and he will feel an inclination to fall over backwards. Inform him that you will be standing behind him and will catch him when he falls. He is perfectly safe and is to let himself go and actually fall right over backwards into your waiting arms, as he feels the impulse pulling him. Further, advise that he is not to try to fall; neither is he to resist falling. He is merely to be relaxed and passive, and is to think of the idea of falling backward which you will give him. Explain, as he does so, that he will experience a very decided drawing sensation pulling him right over backwards; to let himself go and fall. You will catch him; he is safe!

Now, as he stands erect with his feet together, his head up, and hands relaxed at his sides, ask him to close his eyes and relax his body. You can ascertain that he is doing as you directed by placing your hand on his shoulder and pulling him back slightly. If your subject sways back easily he is relaxing correctly.

Then step behind him.

Standing directly behind your subject, place the side of your right forefinger lightly at the base of his brain (at the nape of his neck), and tilt his head backward just a bit, so it rests lightly upon this finger. See Fig. 4.

Now, in a low, monotonous voice suggest, "In a few seconds you will begin to feel an impulse to fall...a sensation of falling right over backward. You are beginning to feel it now. You are beginning to fall-to fall-- to fall right over backwards into my arms. When I withdraw my hand from your head, you will slowly fall back, backwards, right over backwards."

The words you give to a subject in hypnotic experiments are known as "suggestions"– which are ideas that produce an unconscious rather than a conscious response. The correct way to present suggestions is to always speak in a calm, positive tone, without haste, and without raising your voice. Keep your voice kind, but, at the same time, let there be no doubt about your authority and the fact that you expect your suggestions to be obeyed. (In chapter four will be given careful consideration to the factors pertinent to presenting suggestions that influence.)

15

As you present these suggestions of falling over backwards, slowly, very slowly, draw your left hand along the side of his head in a gentle stroking action. Draw it directly back from the subject's temple until if clears the back of his head. At the same time, gradually lighten the pressure of your right forefinger so that he can scarcely feel it touching the nape of his neck.

Continue your suggestions, "Now you feel the influence getting stronger ... it is drawing you back. You are falling backwards .. falling backwards."

Simultaneously, with the giving of these suggestions, continue repeating the sliding of your left fingers in the slow strokings along the side of his head. Gradually, as your subject commences to sway, stroke your left hand clear and free of his head, and in this motion also remove your right hand gently from the nape of his neck, so that your hands are clear behind him and ready to catch him as he falls, as you continue to suggest, "You are falling backwards.. you are falling backwards." See Fig. 5.

As your suggestions thus continue, soon your subject will commence to sway, and will shortly topple over backwards into your arms. As he falls. be sure and catch him, and immediately help him to regain his balance.

Continue right on to this next test without interruption.

Briefly explain that this influence of ideas concentrated on to produce unconscious actions will affect the sense of balance in any direction. Ask your subject this time to stand relaxed facing you, as you show him the next experiment of drawing him over forwards.

Have him look you directly in the eyes, and, as he does this, *fix your own gaze directly upon the root of his nose; looking him straight between his eyes.* This is a bit of technique frequently used by hypnotists. You will find that you can concentrate much better by fixing on one point rather than by trying to look into both of the subject's eyes at the same time. Hypnotists call this "the hypnotic gaze," and as far as the audience and the subject is concerned, it appears that you are looking him directly in the eyes.

At this point, tell your subject to concentrate on your suggestions pulling him over forward this time, and that soon he will find himself falling forwards right towards you, just as he did in falling over backwards in the previous experiment. Now raise your hands and rest them very lightly on each side of his head, as shown in Fig. 6.

Still looking him squarely between the eyes, you allow your fingers to rest thus on his temples for a few seconds in silence, and then, moving your left foot back a step, slowly and very lightly draw your fingers along the sides of his head toward the front, at the same time bending your body backward a bit at the

16

Fig. 4   Fig. 5

hips as your two hands come together in the front of his forehead in this action. Then, slowly separate them, bend forward, and again place your fingers upon the sides of his head repeating the lingering stroking motion along the sides of his head ending in the center of his forehead as previously.

Having performed this forward drawing motion three times, suggest to him impressively, while continuing to keep your gaze intently centered on the root of his nose and observing carefully that his eyes do not wander from yours even for an instant, "Now you feel a drawing impulse causing you to fall forward. Do not resist, I will catch you..Let yourself go. You are coming forward. You falling forward right over towards me."

As you give these suggestions, very slowly draw your hands again forward along the sides of his head, finally drawing them completely clear of his head as you bend slightly backward and downward. . your subject will follow right along and fall directly into your arms See Fig. 7.

Keep a continual barrage of suggestions going in this test, such as:

"You are falling forward. You are falling forward. You are falling forward. When I withdraw my hands from your temples you will fall forward -- right over forward, forward, forward!"

Remember to constantly watch the eyes of your subject. If they remain fixed and intent you can be certain of the experiment succeeding. Such fixity of attention is important in all such experiments. If the subject's eyes waver or wander from yours, stop the test at once and explain that he must keep his gaze riveted upon yours at all times; then proceed with the experiment until he falls directly over into your arms, and at once again help him to regain his balance.

17

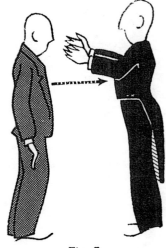

Fig. 6   Fig. 7

Observe William James's theory of "ideo-motor action" in operation in these preliminary tests. They show clearly how an idea of motion centered in the mind leads *unconsciously* to motor action, as noted in the present instance of the idea of falling actually causing the subject to fall.

The subject's own reaction to these experiments is further enlightening. He knows he did not deliberately try to fall over. To him the sensation seemed exactly as if some outside force were actually drawing him, compelling him, pulling on him, causing him to fall. This sensation of an outside force develops because suggestion produces an i n v o l u n t a r y rather a voluntary effect. In actual fact, the influence that causes the subject to fall originates within his own mind and imparts automatic (unconscious) movements to his muscles, which, in turn, cause him to sway in the direction of his thought, and eventually topple over.

At this point, in your first experiments with your preliminary subject(s), you have a good opportunity to explain about "the power of suggestion" and some of the interesting things that can be accomplished through its use. This little story illustrates it well:

Imagine, if you will, that we have a plank of wood about one foot wide and twelve feet long. We place it on the floor of the room and walk along it from one end to the other. You can do this readily and keep your balance perfectly. Its easy. But now let's say we take that very same plank and place it high up in the air, such as between two tall buildings. Can you walk over it now like you did before?

18

Most people refuse even to try. Why? After all, you have just walked along the very same board from one end to the other without the slightest difficulty, why the hestitation now to try it again just because it has been elevated. The matter of balance is still the same.

It is well that you (and other persons) do refuse to walk along the board in its new precarious position, as the chances are you would become dizzy, and possibly take a disastrous fall to the street below.

Again we ask, why?

Because the position of the board, now stretched out over a great height, *suggests* the idea of a fall. Actually, from a physical standpoint, it is no more difficult to keep your balance in walking along the board in its present position bridging two buildings than it was to walk along it on the floor, but from a psychological standpoint the situation has been greatly altered. *The suggestion of falling* is now present, and it is so powerful that it decidedly interferes with one's sense of balance. And reason about it as you will, you cannot overcome the suggestion (fear) of the idea of a dangerous fall!

This story-example will quickly illustrate to your subject (s) just what the "power of suggestion" is and how it operates unconsciously. The explanation is clear and will put him in a receptive mood to learn more, and try further experiments.

It is well for both the hypnotist and the subject to understand the operation of suggestion for it is the basis of hypnosis. For this understanding, bear in mind that suggestions are ideas which, when centered in the mind (concentrated upon), stimulate the imagination and lead to an active, automatic response. In other words, suggestive ideas, once they go into action, produce *involuntary* effects.

You are now ready to propose another preliminary test to your subject.

Request him to again look fixedly into your eyes and under no circumstances to remove his gaze from yours. Now, stretch your hands out toward him, palms upward, and tell him to grasp your hands tightly. As he does this, bend your head forward a little until it is within six inches of his own. The position is shown in Fig. 8.

After holding this position for about ten seconds, suggest very positively, "you fill find now that you cannot unclasp your hands. You cannot take them away from mine. They are fastened to mine so tightly that you cannot move them. The muscles of your arms and hands are rigid and tight. Your hands are stuck tightly to mine. Try and take your hands away. Try hard, but

19

Fig. 8

you cannot, for they are stuck tightly to mine!"

If your subject is following your suggestions with earnest concentration, his hands will become tightly locked to yours. He will pull and struggle, and be entirely unable to release his grip.

You can tell by his eyes how intently he is concentrating on your suggestions. His gaze must be fixed and earnest, and when the suggestions are being accepted, when he starts to pull and yet finds that his hands continue to cling to yours despite his efforts, you will note a shadow of a puzzled expression creep into his eyes. Hammer home your suggestions even more forcefully at this point, as you exclaim "See, your hands are stuck, they are stuck so tightly to mine that you cannot release them you cannot pull them away no matter how hard you try. Try, try hard! They will not come free . . they are stuck, stuck tight!"

After your subject has tried in vain to release his hands from yours for a few seconds, say, "All right. It is alright, you can relax your hands now. Relax. Relax your hands. You can now release them. Your hands are free."

Obeying these suggestions, your subject will immediately be able to unlock his grip.

You are learning how to skillfully use the power of suggestion. The successful induction of the experiment just described requires a deeper degree of concentration than the previous tests. In your experimenting, be certain to use the three preliminary tests here given, in the order presented, as they have been arranged for ease of execution, *and succeed with each test you perform with your subject (s) before carrying on to the next.*

3

Experiments in
Waking Suggestion

Some psychologists refer to the phenomena you are now studying as waking hypnosis, others as waking suggestion. I personally prefer the latter term as it keeps tests of this nature distinct from the more advanced hypnotic experiments you will subsequently learn.

Beginning students of hypnotism often seem surprised at the fact that it is possible to produce striking hypnotic effects in the waking state, independent of what is known as "the hypnotic trance." Basically, suggestive influence in the waking state is not different from suggestive influence in the hypnotic state except in degree of intensity. Further, tests in waking suggestion have a usefulness in gradually "conditioning" your subject(s) for achieving successfully the deeper experiments in hypnosis that will be performed.

The experiment you will first learn in this chapter was developed by the eminent French psychologist, Emile Coue early in this century, and was used by him to demonstrate *the power of suggestion.* It has become a classic in the repertoire of many hypnotists.

Locking the Subject's Hands Together

If you have succeeded in effectively fastening your subject's hands to yours, as described in the last chapter, you are now ready for this test which is unquestionably the nost important of any you have performed thus far. If you succeed in this experiment with the subject, you can be almost certain of achieving success in all manner of waking suggestions effects of the muscular variety. Indeed, response to this test can often be used as a means of judging a subject's response to suggestion generally, and measuring his potential for being a successful hypnotic subject. Learn to perform it well.

Have your subject stand facing you, and again look directly into your eyes. Under no circumstances is he to remove his gaze. Then request him to extend his arms out straight in front of himself and clasp his hands together with the fingers interlocked. Ask him to push his hands as tightly together as he possibly can, to make his arms stiff and rigid, and to think he cannot take his hands apart by repeating over and over mentally the suggestions, "I cannot get my hands apart, I cannot get my hands apart, I cannot get my hands apart!"

Now stretch out your hands towards him and clasp his locked hands in yours pressing on them firmly. Keep your eyes fixed on him in the "hypnotic gaze" manner, which you have learned. Keep your gaze rapt and watch your subject's eyes. If they remain fixed and centered then he is concentrating as directed, but if they waver and shift, command him not to look away, but to keep his gaze firm and steady as he concentrates on the suggestions. See Fig. 9.

Now say to the subject in a positive tone, "You will find your hands are sticking together tight, tighter, tighter, tight, and you cannot take them apart. You cannot unclasp your hands, they are stuck tightly together, they will not come apart, they are stuck tight, tight, tight!"

As you give these suggestions continue pressing on the subject's clasped hands, pressing them tighter and tighter together. Now, remove your hands, thus giving the subject a chance to test the influence as you continue:

"You will find the muscles of your hands and arms are so rigid and stiff that your hands simply will not come apart. You cannot budge them. They are stuck tight together, stuck tight! Try and take your hands apart. Try hard. PULL! Pull with all your might. They will not come, they are stuck tight together."

If your subject has been following your suggestions with earnest concentration, his hands will have become so tightly locked together, that tug and struggle as he will, he simply cannot pull his locked hands apart.

In giving these suggestions, remember to speak positively, slowly, and distinctly, becoming continuously more and more forceful .. and throw more and more energy and command into the suggestions until the climax is reached when the subject is challenged that he cannot take his hands apart. Such is the way to give suggestions that influence.

As soon as your subject has tried in vain to release his hands, snap your fingers beside his ear and suggest, "All right now, the influence is all gone. Relax. You can take your hands apart now."

Immediately, the concentration being broken, he will find that he can separate his hands.

Occasionally the subject's hands will have become so tightly locked together they will not separate even when you tell him to relax and take them apart. In such instance, simply take his hands gently in your own, and softly suggest, "All right, it's all right. Relax your hands now. I will count slowly from one to three, and at the count of 'three' your hands will come right apart."

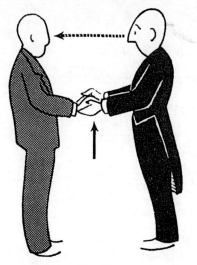

Fig. 9   Fig. 10

Then count, "One, two, three," and at the count of "three," suddenly clap your hands together, and his hands will then easily unclasp. See Fig. 10.

Having successfully performed the foregoing test, immediately, using the same subject, you may go directly into the performance of these further experiments:

Stiffening the Subject's Leg

Ask your subject to place his weight on his left leg, while you take hold of his right hand. Tell him to look you straight in the eyes, and to hold the idea firmly in his mind that he will be unable to bend his leg. Impress on him that his eyes must follow yours under all conditions.

Now make a few passes down his leg with your hands, commencing about six inches above the knee, and press in lightly on the knee joint. While making these passes, suggest positively, "Now you will find your leg is getting stiff -- stiffer -- stiffer -- stiff -- and you cannot bend it. The knee joint is getting so stiff you cannot bend it. You can feel the muscles in your leg getting more and more rigid. It is impossible for you to bend your leg. IT IS STIFF, STIFF, STIFF! Try to bend it. You cannot do it! Try, try hard!" See Fig. 11.

As you say these last words, rise up slowly, keeping your gaze centered at the root of your subject's nose, and pull him toward you actually causing him to walk stiff-legged.

When he has walked some steps on his stiff leg, remove the influence by clapping your hands together as you say, "All right, the influence is all gone now. You can bend your leg. It is all loose and free."

Stiffening the Subject's Arm

Ask your subject to hold his arm outstretched, close his hand into a tight fist, and make his arm very stiff as he holds it out straight in front of himself. Now, take hold of his fist and make a few passes down the insides of the arm, as you suggest:

Your arm is getting stiff, stiff, stiffer, stiffer, very stiff. You cannot bend it. Try hard, but it is so stiff that the harder you try to bend it, the stiffer it becomes. It is impossible to bend it! Try hard, but you cannot bend your arm no matter how hard you try."

The subject will try hard, but is totally unable to bend his arm. Remove the effects of the suggestions again by clapping your hands and suggesting, "Relax now, the influence is all gone. Relax! You can easily bend your arm now."

In performing all of these tests in waking suggestion (in the waking state of mind), make certain that your subject's gaze is always intent upon you. *This is very important.* You will find that as you proceed from test to test, and as your subject responds successfully to each, that you may conduct each test more and more rapidly, until often just a few decisive suggestions will obtain the desired results.

Your experiments in waking suggestion may now become of a more involved sort, of which the following is an excellent example:

Fastening a Stick to the Subject's Hands

Have your subject stand before you and tightly grip a broom handle or a cane. He is to grip the stick with his fingers below and thumbs on tops, as shown in Fig. 12.

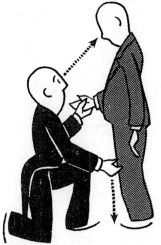

Fig. 11   Fig. 12

Tell the subject to think intently on the fact that he cannot let go of the stick, and that he will find, when you count "Three." that he cannot throw it down no matter how hard he tries, and that the harder he tries to throw it from himself, the more the stick will cling to his hands.

Then suggest, "Ready, one.....two.......three! .... Now you cannot throw the stick down. Try. Try hard. You cannot throw it down; the more you try, the more it sticks to your hands."

Suddenly clap your hands and say, "All right, you can let go of it now. Throw the stick down!"

Your subject will throw the offending stick from himself with vengeance.

Producing the Inability of the Subject to Sit Down

In this test, have the subject stand in front of a chair which is placed directly behind him. Request him to gaze into your eyes, tell him to make his legs stiff, and to think that he cannot sit down no matter how hard he tries: that when you count "three" (such counting is used as a *cue* for the response to occur at a specific time in giving suggestions) he will find that his legs have become so stiff and rigid that he cannot sit down, and the more he tries to sit down the more impossible he will find it to do so." (In such suggestion handling, you are applying what is known as "the law of reversed effort," i.e., in direct ratio to the effort put forth in definance of the suggestions does the effect of the suggestions increase.)

Then suggest, "Ready, One, two, three ———— now you cannot sit down. Your legs are stiff, your body is stiff, you cannot sit down. Try to sit down, try hard, but you cannot!"

After the subject has tried to sit in vain for a few seconds, remove the influence by clapping your hands quickly and saying, "All right, it's all gone now. you can sit down easily. The influence is all gone."

Producing the Inability of the Subject to Stand Up

Have the subject sit in a chair and look upwards into your eyes, as you suggest:

"You are getting stuck in that chair. You're glued to the seat. Think hard on how stiff your muscles are; how tightly stuck you are to the seat of that chair. You can't get up. You are stuck to the seat. I will count from one to three, at the count of three you will find you cannot rise out of that chair no matter how hard you try. You are stuck tightly to the seat of that chair. Ready. One, two, three. See, you are stuck!

You try to get up, but you cannot! Try. Try hard to get up. It is impossible!"

I wish to train you well in this use of waking suggestion as it is important to your success as a hypnotic entertainer. In your performance you will be using such feats of waking state phenomena, so master these tests well.

If you have succeeded in the tests up to this point, you will find that you can readily influence the subject(s) in all such types of experiments using waking suggestion. These are numerous.

A little imagination on your part will suggest many possibilities for effective tests, such as fastening the subject's mouth closed so he cannot open it, placing his hand flat on the floor so that it is impossible for him to pull free, sticking his feet in position so he cannot walk, etc. In performing all of these tests, the principle and application is mainly the same: (a) fixing the subject's attention acutely on yourself by having him look directly into your eyes, while you gaze back at him directly between his eyes at the root of his nose, and (b) concentrating the subject's attention upon the barrage of respective suggestions which you hammer home into his mind by positive repetition of the various effects you wish to accomplish. Likewise, as your experiments in waking suggestion become more involved, there occurs what hypnotists refer to as "the confusion technique." This is produced by heaping the influence of one suggestion response upon another, ad finitum. The bewilderment of the subject in finding himself unable to perform one set of actions leads to confusion so the mind readily accepts and responds to subsequent suggestions. Confusion leads to more confusion, and the suggestions are accepted uncritically and automatically acted upon.

Unless the student has observed or experienced the influence of suggestion personally, it is difficult to fully appreciate, through the written work, just how verbal commands -- such as these -- can produce these effects. In relation to hypnotic influence, remember that it is not the words being spoken that are important, but rather the ideas such convey, and that the response of the subject to these ideas is not a voluntary one; the actions of the subject being entirely involuntary as your flow of suggestions take hold of the unconscious side of his mind, and directs its responses quite independent of his will.

To illustrate the point, recall again the incident of trying to walk over that board stretched out between two tall buildings. The more a person tried in vain to counteract fears of a fall in crossing over the board, and the more he tried not to fall, the more he felt that surely he would fall.

Of such is the operation of suggestion.

Or, consider the case of a man obsessed by stage fright. He fears that he may get tongue-tied and be unable to speak well, so he reasons with himself that he has nothing to fear, that talking to a large crowd is no more difficult that talking to one person. He tries to assure himself that he will be able to talk clearly and freely before the audience. He is thus trying to use his will.

But imagination steps in and takes over; comes the time for his speech before the group, his imagined difficulties (suggestions) crop up and completely eclipse his good intentions. And the more he tries to speak well, the more he blunders and develops an embarrassing case of stage fright.

Of such is the operation of suggestion.

Which brings us to one of the basic laws of suggestion: When the Imagination and the Will are in conflict, the imagination invariably wins the day.

You will begin to appreciate the power that exists in suggestive ideas. Illustrations of its operation are about us constantly -- selling and advertising are excellent examples. These forces constantly endeavor to appeal to our emotions, to stimulate our imaginations, and implant desires. And when successful, the culmination of our aroused desire becomes an automatic response. Fortunately, all suggestive ideas do not take root in our mind. If they did, life would be a very complicated place indeed, and we would be buffeted about from one suggestion to another without a vestige of will of our own. For in actual fact, ninety-nine out of a hundred of the ideas that are presented to us do not carry enough of an emotional wallop, as it were, to stimulate our imagination to the extent that they become sufficiently centered in our attention to give rise to unconscious (automatic) effects, or else they are defeated by countersuggestions already in force in our mind. Obviously, the vast majority of suggestions are rejected, or kept within the realm of reason. That is where your skill as a hypnotist comes in, for you must give your suggestions in such a manner that they will tend to arouse an emotional response and excite the imagination.

Some people are quite resistant to the effect of suggestion, so naturally you cannot expect to influence every person you experiment on, especially at the very beginning of your training in the art.

Quite possibly you may influence and hypnotize the very first person you work with, or you may fail with the first half dozen or more, but consider it all under the heading of experience and perserverance. Simply be courteous and never show any disappointment at failure. If you have difficulty, merely remark that it isn't possible to hypnotize everyone at the very first trial, and proceed on with your work.

There is a knack in giving suggestion so that they will produce hypnotic effects which comes only from practice and experience. Patience and perseverance will bring this skill. Sooner or later you will succeed in *hypnotizing someone, and that very first*

27

subject is a very important milestone in your progress as a hypnotist; you will be amazed at the insight it gives you towards the ability of giving suggestions that hypnotize. And here's a very important tip to keep in mind when you present such suggestions, viz.:

When you state, as an example, that your subject's hands are fastened so tightly together that he connot pull them apart, in your own mind visualize the image of his hands being so locked together and see him (in your mind's eye) pulling in vain to separate them. Don't have the slightest doubt but that the experiment will occur exactly as you command it. Forget all ideas of failure. KNOW that your suggestions will be followed. Such conviction does wonders for your manner, tone, and delivery in producing positive suggestions.

Learning how to present suggestions that influence is so important to your training in professional hypnotism that I am devoting the entire next chapter to the matter to give you further instruction and further stress the principles you have been mastering.

4
Presenting Suggestions
That Influence

Suggestions can carry an amazing amount of influence; an incident is told of a college student who was killed by its power. At a fraternity initation he was blindfolded, and, after the usual emotion arousing proceedings, was told that he was to have his head chopped off. His head was then placed on the block, and viciously the knife slashed into his neck. It was actually only a wet towel, but the victim died -- of heart failure. His subconscious had accepted the idea that the knife was real, and when the cold towel desended it ended his life just as surely as death would have followed a genuine decapitation.

The fact that suggestion can produce physical responses in our body can be easily proved by simply thinking of a juicy, sour, bitter lemon; feel how spontaneously the thought starts the flow of saliva within your mouth. Or think of itchy sensations about your body, and feel those itches commence.

But surely, it will be questioned, not every person who takes part in a college initiation, such as above described, would die as the result of a damp towel striking across his neck? The answer I have already given you in this study, but as it is important I will repeat the concept here of this basic law in the operation of this power, viz.:

Every suggestive idea which enter the consciousness, *if it is accepted by the subconsciousness,* is automatically transformed by it into a reality and becomes an element in our life.

In that qualifying phrase lies the heart of the power of suggestion: *if it is accepted by the subconscious.* The laws of applied suggestion impose, 1. the acceptance of the idea (suggestion), 2. its transformation into a reality. Both of these operations are performed automatically by the subconscious aspect of mind, if the idea carries enough power to drive it home into the subconscious. The operation of unconscious behavior is such that every idea, if it is subconsciously accepted, must go spontaneously into effect. Whether the idea originates with the mind of the subject or from outside source is a matter of inconsequence. In both instances, the idea undergoes precisely the same function: it is submitted (via suggestion) to the subconscious, accepted or rejected, and so either realized or ignored.

To the stage hypnotist, it is important that his suggestions be accepted, and there are certain basic ways of presenting suggestions that make them most effective, viz.:

Timing. Paramount among these is the proper timing of the suggestions presented. In other words, you do not usually want to tell the subject that something is happening before it has happened. Andre Weitzenhoffer[2] expresses this effectively. " A good rule is that if you see indications that a certain event is going to take place at any moment, then you can suggest that it is taking place. Otherwise, and probably this is perferable in all cases, you should introduce the event as a future possibility and work up, more or less gradually, to making a positive statement of its presence."

Reptition. Reptition in the giving of suggestions is also important. It is cumulative in its effect; prevents the hypnotist from getting ahead too fast and out of proper timing in giving his suggestions to the subject, as well as having a certain monotony about it that is, in itself, hypnotic in effect.

Delivery. Proper delivery of the suggestions is, likewise, fundamental to their acceptance. In this regard, tone, inflection, and phrasing all have their places -- the major purpose of all being to focus the subject's attention on the suggested phenomena at all times. There are instances when a rapid-fire barrage of suggestions is indicated; conversely there are times when a slower pace of insistence will prove most effective. There are times when it is well to challenge the subject to try to resist the influence. The very inability the subject finds in not being able to do so enforcing the effect of the suggestion. And there are times when the very opposite of challenging is desired, an earnest persuasion providing the best suggestion.

Here are additional means of increasing the influence of suggestions:

Combining of Suggestions. This makes for a most effective demonstration as well as increasing the influence. An example of this handling will be observed in "The Hand Clasping Test," which you have learned how to perform. In this test, the subject is told that his arm muscles are becoming tight and rigid, that his fingers are interlocked and cramped, and that his hands are clasped together so tightly that he cannot pull them apart no matter how hard he tries. Notice how each suggestion used in combination reinforces the next building towards the desired response of the hands being locked together. This combining of suggestions is an important principle to apply in many suggestive situations.

Training the Subject in Suggestive Responsiveness. Every individual has a certain potential to the influence of suggestion. This varies in different persons and may be increased or decreased by training through a graduating response to suggestions. If the suggestions succeed, the suggestibility ratio is increased; if they fail, the reverse is the case. For this reason, it is often well to train subjects in successful suggestive responsiveness by allowing them to proceed from simplier tests on towards the more difficult. The principle of graduated suggestive responsiveness is observed in operation in the hypnotism show by the commencing on to the complete induction of hypnosis. Refining it even further, even the gradual performance of the simplier on to the more complex waking suggestion experiments is desirable. I have followed this procedure exactly in instructing you in this textbook.

Voluntary Actions to Increase Suggestibility. A voluntary response to a suggestion has an influence in increasing the response to an involuntary one. In practical application to the hypnotist, the use of this principle lies in instructing the subject to do certain things that he must comply with before presenting actual hypnotic suggestions. For example, telling him to stand at a certain place, holding a certain position, moving from here to there. sitting down, standing up, placing his feet flat on the floor, resting his hands in his lap in a certain way, doing this or doing that, as the case may be, in relation to the performance. Obedience to such commands tends to cause the subject to act upon your suggestions uncritically which has a carry-over effect to the acceptance of the subsequent hynotic suggestions.

Deep Breathing to Increase Suggestibility. This is a further refinement of a voluntary action increasing suggestibility, in this instance, deep breathing being the voluntary action requested by the performer. The late Konradi Leitner used this technique effectively and made use of it in his handling of "The Hand Locking Test." This experienced hypnotist would combine his suggestions of muscular rigidity with instructions to inhale and exhale rhythmically. The effect of this was to transfer a voluntary action (breathing) over to the involuntary one of the hands becomming locked together; each process reinforcing the other.

I make use of this breathing in unison procedure in conjunction with my induction technique for mass stage hypnotizing, as you will subsequently be instructed.

The Counting Technique. It is an effective process, and one frequently employed by stage hypnotists to suggest to the subject, "At the count of three you will do so and so. One . . two . . . three!" And the suggestion will occur at such and such a time -- on cue, as it were -- often intensifies the suggestive influence.

Nonverbal Suggestions. These consist of all suggestive influences exerted by the performer other than verbal suggestions, i.e., such processes as gestures, body movements, breathing, pantomine, etc. As an example, the forward or backward movement of the

31

body in performing "Postural Sway Experiments," or the gestures of the hands in passes inwards towards the face of the subject carry such suggestive influence. The use of nonverbal suggestions are very important to the hypnotist, and their use should be developed to become an associated part of his suggestive pattern combined with verbal suggestions.

Mass (Group) Suggestions. The use of suggestion upon a group is frequently more readily performed than when working with a solo subject. The element of self-consciousness is eliminated when being part of a crowd; also the factor of imitation is present. Seeing the suggestion working upon others is a strong factor in accepting its working upon oneself. Mass suggestion is of vital usage to the stage hypnotist.

As to exactly how the operator is to know which suggestive approach it is best to use on a particular subject, there is no precise answer. It is well to appreciate these rules of effectively presenting suggestions that influence, and then strive intelligently to bring them into application. Experience will be your best teacher.

I will now give you some further refinement of information relative to effective presenting suggestions that influence. As an example, suppose in the presence of several people I crack and break open a perfectly fresh egg. As I do this, I make a wry face and exclaim "Whew this egg smells rotten. I wouldn't eat it for a hundred dollars." Now pass the egg around and let everyone smell it. Some of the people present will agree that the perfectly good egg has a most offensive odor; others will agree that it even looks bad.

In the above example, these people have been temporarily persuaded to accept an idea that the fresh egg is bad. They most certainly have not been placed into a trance, yet through these suggestions they are exhibiting true hypnotic phenomena. *Suggestion will be seen to be the key for inducing the hypnotic state as well as the means of its control.*

It will be observed by the student that many of the effects obtainable in deep hypnosis may also be produced in waking hypnosis (waking suggestion). Indeed, through your skill at using waking suggestion will come your skill in presenting suggestions that influence, which will lead to complete mastery of the art of hypnotizing.

Consider the case of "the egg that smelled rotten." You made a positive statement (a suggestion) of apparent fact which your listeners accepted as fact. You by-passed their critical factors, substituting your own. Respect for your judgement caused them to believe what you said even before they smelled the egg. Thus, having minimized their ability to judge the egg fairly, you asked

32

them to judge the egg. They judged the egg, not with their own critical faculties, but with yours. They were in a state of mind in which your judgement superseded theirs. You gave them an illusion that a good egg was a bad egg. While you have not produced formal hypnosis in any sense, you have definitely produced hypnotic phenomena, which clearly shows the close overlap of waking suggestion with deeper trance states.

Throughout all experiments with suggestion and hypnosis, it will be noticed how the critical factor of the mind is by-passed and a substitute judgement used. Observe these psychological rules:

1. The mind of the subject must be locked around a given idea.

2. To cause the mind of a subject to become locked around a given idea, suggestions must be given with complete confidence and absolute assurance. Present the suggestions in a manner that implies that what you have said is as inevitable   the rising of the sun.

3. For a suggestion to be effective, it must be presented in such a way that the suggestion will be accepted without causing the critical faculties of the mind to be brought into action. For this purpose, the fine use of language (sematics) is extremely important to the hypnotist. It is in the way he phrases his suggestions and the way in which he presents them that his skill as a master hypnotist developes. Such handling brings consent, and consent (be it conscious or unconscious) is always necessary in any hypnotic effect.

Words are your major means of conveying suggestions to your subject. Words are triggers to action that automatically release mental sets (learned responses unconscious reactions) in the mind of the listener. It has been said that the proper word spoken in the right way at the right time can change the world. As a hypnotist, you must learn to use words well and appreciate their power!

4. For a suggestion to be effective in a hypnotic sense, it must be one that the subject wants and/or believes possible, or at least doesn't object to. If you give a suggestion that is objectionable, the critical faculties of the mind are brought into play, and the suggestion will be minimized. Suggestions which play upon the subject's wants are always those most acceptable.

By way of illustration, a person suffering pain wants relief. Such a person is apt to quickly accept the suggestion for alleviation of his distress, but will resist suggestions that would bring on more. Let the subject hear the words which he is anxious to hear. Do not tell him that he will not hurt anymore, as such brings critical factors to bear, rather frame your suggestions in some manner such as this, "Now that you are relaxed, you will find that what bothered you a moment ago is much better now. In fact, it ceases to bother you any further. Close your eyes for a moment, it will help you relax. Now, when you open your eyes hold on to your relaxation, and nothing will disturb you further. Open your eyes and notice how good you feel."

Such is the way of the trained suggestive therapist. And the technique works because the subject's mind becomes locked around an idea to which he is receptive. This applies to the use of suggestion as also does it apply to all conditions and situations you will meet in the conduct of your everyday affairs. Be positive and confident, lock the mind of the person you wish to influence around your ideas, and you will be successful.

The use of these principles of waking hypnosis apply strongly on the stage, and also in all directions of life. If you are an executive, a businessman, or a salesman, remember that when the prospect comes to you, he is already receptive to your sales talk. He is in a consent state, ready to be convinced (influenced). "Waking suggestion," in this sense, is responsible for ninety percent of all sales . Your expert knowledge and use of waking suggestion will result in increased prosperity for you in business, as well as in your success as a hypnotic showman upon the stage.

As a conclusion to this chapter, I will show you how to perform an interesting experiment in waking suggestion upon your subject, which, also, serves nicely as a transition into the instructions for producing the hypnotic trance.

Fastening the Subject's Eyelids Together

Ask your subject to be seated, and while standing in front of him and a little to one side, tell him to raise his eyes to yours and to concentrate on them When he has gazed in this manner for approximately ten seconds, gently close his eyelids with your fingertips, and resting your other hand on his wrist pulse, tell him to continue to look upwards underneath his closed eyelids. See Fig. 13.

Now, say to him very slowly and impressively, "Your eyes are becoming stuck together. The lids are stuck tight. They will not open. Your eyes are stuck shut. You cannot open your eyes, try as hard as you will. You cannot open them. Try hard. Hard! See, they are stuck tight, they will not open."

As you give the above suggestions, place the thumb of your right hand on the subject's forehead just above the bridge of his nose and press downward.

Your subject will in vain struggle to open his eyes, but he simply cannot do so. His eyebrows will rise and fall, but the eyelids will remain tightly shut. Having made several ineffectual attempts to open them suddenly remove your thumb from the center of his forehead, snap you fingers by his ear, and say, "All right, the influence is all gone ... you can open your eyes now."

The subject's eyes will pop open with a surprised expression.

Step by step, you and your subject have thus practiced the effects of suggestion on the mind, and you are both now ready to try for hypnosis.

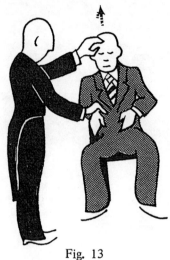

Fig. 13

5
How to Hypnotize

Thus far all of your hypnotic experiments have been conducted in the waking state, which may be regarded as being representative, more or less, as our normal mental state. You are now ready to deal with an *altered* state of mind. As the hypnotizing process makes use of suggestions of "sleep," and sleep is an unconscious condition, it used to be believed that hypnosis produced unconsciousness. However, subsequent experiments by psychologists have shown hypnosis to be more closely allied to consciousness than it is to sleep, so it is no longer felt that in being hypnotized the subject becomes unconscious. This does not imply, however, that the hypnotized person is in the same state of mind as that common to everyday experience, *as hypnosis is something unique in itself and very wonderful.*

You will learn more of this when you study the theory of hypnotism, in chapter eleven of this book. For our immediate practical purpose of learning how to hypnotize, it will suffice to consider it simply as a state of mind of acute attention in which the effects of suggestions are greatly amplified.

In experimenting with your subject or subjects, as the case may be, you can explain that being hypnotized does not make a person unconscious, they will very possibly know what is going on, but occurrences will seem rather remote like a dream experience, and like a pleasant dream all experiences will be pleasurable.

This explanation will be found helpful as many people have a fear of losing consciousness completely, also you can mention that entering hypnosis is an entirely harmless experience that will be thoroughly enjoyed, and that the relaxation produced will actually do the subject a great deal of good.

Then ask if he is willing to be hypnotized, and advise that he must concentrate his entire attention upon all of your suggestions. Tell him not to resist, to just let himself go, and willingly place himself in your hands with confidence as you conduct this experiment in hypnotism together.

These pretrance *(I use the term, trance, in the classic sense of being the condition of mind known as hypnosis. In this text, trance and hypnosis are to be regarded as synonymous.)* instructions are most important, for to make the experiment a success there must exist a feeling and trust and cooperation between the subject and the hypnotist.

This first method of hypnotizing, in which I will instruct you, is very thorough, and while it is not as rapid as some of the other methods which will be described later in this book, during your apprentice period you will find it a wise one to apply both from the standpoints of teaching you details of the technique as well as the effective influence it will have upon many of the subjects with whom you practice. It is genteel and pleasant.

I call this "The Fixation Method of Hypnotizing" as the subject's eyes are first centered upon a small object to concentrate upon. For this purpose any small, bright object may be used. I personally use a clear glass marble; this device is technically known as a "fixation object."

In using a fixation object to hypnotize, the glass marble is held between your thumb and fingers, and with a rotating motion of the hand is revolved around and around in a small three inch circle. Being bright it will capture the light and hold attention. Hold the marble up in front of your subject in a position that will make his eyes strain upward a bit to look at it. Continue this rotating motion until the eyes of your subject close, then place the little ball aside.

Your subject prepared to be hypnotized, ask him to take a seat in a comfortable chair and to relax well back. Have him adjust himself so he will be entirely comfortable and will not have to move about. Then hold the "fixation object" six or seven inches in front of his eyes, requesting that he watch it intently while allowing his eyes to follow its rotary motion, and to think of sleep. See Fig. 14.

You then continue rotating the little glass ball around and around for four or five minutes, until your subject's eyes close. And while revolving it, repeat the following suggestions in a low, monotonous, positive tone of voice:

"Your eyelids will soon begin to feel very heavy. Concentrate your gaze on the 'fixation object' and follow it around and around and around. It makes your eyes become so heavy; your eyes are getting tired; they are getting moist; they are beginning to wink. You cannot see distinctly any longer. Your eyelids are getting so heavy, they want to close. Your eyelids are closing." Repeat these suggestions as is necessary to close your subject's eyes. In the event that his eyes do not close after a reasonable time, directly request, "Close your eyes tightly now and go sound asleep."

Next place your hands on the subject's head so your thumbs rest together in the center of his forehead just above the eyes, and your fingers lie along each side of his head, as shown in Fig. 15. Now move your thumbs slowly from the center of the forehead outward over the temples in a gentle stroking motion, and repeat this process for two or three minutes. Keep your fingers still, just moving the thumbs, as you say, "Sleep ...sleepy sleepy . . sleep -- sound sleep . . sleep . . sleepy sleep". Speak in

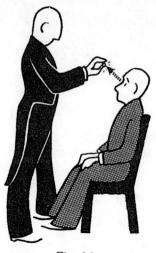

Fig. 14   Fig. 15

a slow, monotonous tone suggestive of sleep. Continue these suggestions of sleep along with this stroking action for a few minutes.

Then place the fingers of your left hand on top of the subject's head, with the thumb of the hand resting on his temple. Leave the fingers of your right hand resting along side of the subject's head just as they were at first, and place the right thumb in the center of his forehead immediately under the hair line. Move this thumb down from his hair line over the center of his forehead slowly until it reaches a little below the bridge of his nose. Vary these stroking motions of your right thumb occasionally by stroking all the way down to the tip of the nose. In making these thumb strokes keep the fingers still. Repeat the process of moving the thumb down the center of the subject's forehead for three or four minutes, and during the entire process continue on giving suggestions of, "Sleep... sleepy ... sleep... sleep... etc." See Fig. 16.

Now move your left thumb from the subject's temple to the root of his nose, between the eyes, leaving the fingers still resting on top of his head, and with your right hand begin to stroke downward over his hair from the back part of the top of the subject's head on down to the base of his brain. Fig. 17 shows the action.

Make these passes slowly, using a firm pressure, all the while continuing to give suggestions of, "Sleep... you are going sound to sleep... asleep ... deep, deep to sleep." Continue, thus, these downward passes over the back of the subject's head for three or four minutes along with the suggestions of "going to sleep."

Standing on the right side of your subject, with your left hand still resting in its previous position on his head as in Fig. 18, repeat the following "sleep formula" in low, positive, monotonous tones (let the monotony of your voice be like the ticking of a clock):

"Your eyes are closed tightly and you cannot open them. Your arms feel heavy. Your hands are motionless. You cannot move. You cannot feel anything. Everything is dark to you. You are going sound asleep   sleep...sleepy...sound asleep...sound asleep ... sound asleep. Your head feels heavy, your limbs feel like lead ... you are so sleepy. When I count three, you will go into a deep, deep sleep. One, two, *three*. You are sound asleep."

Now start at the beginning of this "sleep formula" and repeat it again; continue the process of repetition over and over for five minutes or so. Occasionally, you can continue it to advantage for as long as ten or even fifteen minutes.

By the end of thirty minutes for this first hypnotic session, if your subject is not seemingly asleep (in hypnosis) discontinue the work for that session, and try it again at a later period.

As was mentioned, this method of hypnotizing is slow and methodical, but your are learning your art so there is no hurry. Just take your time; it is good practice for you. This is a very soothing method and you will find it will influence a great many of the subjects on whom you practice.

As you develop your skill in hypnotizing, many of your subjects will go in trance in but a few minutes, in which case you can discontinue the long process of repeating the "sleep formula" over and over. And, as your results continue to improve, of course the length of time you give to each successive step in the

Fig. 16

Fig. 17

40

Fig. 18

process may be shortened until this method of inducing hypnosis need not exceed more than five minutes or so all inclusive.

Its fun to hypnotize, both you and your subject will enjoy it.

Let us pause in your practice of hypnotizing to analyze briefly, step by step, this induction method as it is important that you have complete knowledge of the modus operandi.

Step One. This is the fixation stage in which the subject relaxing in his chair gazes fixedly upon the object. The attention is captured and held, and suggestions are presented that result in body relaxation and eyelid closure.

Step Two. The next processes of this method employ a variety of tactile hypnotic passes on the subject. This contact is very gentle and soothing, and is hypnotic in effect. The techniques described are expertly designed, learn them well. Simultaneously with the contact passes, a "sleep formula" is given.

Step Three. The "sleep formula" consists of a grouping of suggestions designed to present ideas of sleep, going to sleep, etc. As sleep in a natural state of mind with which everyone is intimately familiar, the one word, "sleep," in itself, is highly suggestive in effect.

Step Four. This is the "sleep" stage, The repeated suggestions -- over and over – of sleep produces a sleep response in the subject, and you will outwardly observe symptoms of sleep occurring such as slumping of posture in the chair, deepening breathing, and complete relaxation.

Physically the subject will seem to be sleeping, but mentally the condition is different. Suggestions of sleep will produce natural sleep in some cases if the subject is left to himself, but in hypnotizing the subject's attention is kept active throughout, and attention is a characteristic of awakeness. *In other words, in inducing hypnosis, while the subject is responding automatically to the idea of going to sleep, his attention is kept busy.* The result of this unusual situation is that rather than the subject going to sleep, as it were, he goes into a condition of *somnambulism.* Somnambulism is the state of mind which in nature occurs in instances of "sleep walking" and "sleep talking." While it is akin to sleep, it is actually an altered consciousness state characterized by heightened suggestibility and accented responsiveness to suggestions. This somnambulistic state of mind is the condition known as hypnosis.

Frequently there will be a loss of memory of hypnotic experiences upon "awakening" from deep hypnosis, this is not caused by recovery from unconsciousness, but is the result of the shifting from one level of consciousness to another which the hypnotic state produces. Also this amnesia effect can be the product of suggestions from the hypnotist that the subject will not remember his experiences in the trance. The subject responds to the suggestions and it seems to him that he has been asleep; in other words, in responding to such suggestions the subject blots out the memory of his experiences and they cease to be recalled. Conversely, suggestions of recall will immediately bring back full memory of all hypnotic experiences intact.

The important point to bear in mind about the hypnotic condition is that it is an induced mental state characterized by *hypersuggestibility.*

The student will be interested in learning as to how one can determine whether or not a subject has reached the somnambulistic stage. A simple physical method of judging is this:

When the subject appears deeply entranced, pick up the subject's right hand from his lap and start revovling it around and around in a circle. Make no verbal comment as you do this, just continue right on presenting the "sleep formula." Having revolved the hand, thus, for thirty seconds or so, release it. If it continues of itself revolving around and around, you may judge that the subject is in hypnosis.

6
A Variety of
Hypnotic Methods

In this chapter, we will discuss some further methods of hypnotizing, including my personal method. You will find these valuable additions to your knowledge as they will equip you with four excellent techniques for inducing hypnosis.

It is well to learn a variety of methods of hypnotizing as they each instruct in different procedures. Gradually you will learn to combine the techniques you prefer and develop your own method. This is where creativity comes in, and you become an artist.

1. The John Kappas Method:

This process will be found useful in affecting people who find it difficult to concentrate their attention upon the idea of sleep as applied in the previous chapter. The essential thing about Mr. Kappas' method is that it provides activity to hold the subject's attention throughout, his technique being that as the hypnotist counts the subject opens and closes his eyes continuously, keeping in time with the counting.

Have your subject seat himself in a comfortable position, and explain to him that you want him to go to sleep. After he has become passive, have him look directly into your eyes, while you gaze intently at the root of his nose (using the "hypnotic gaze," as you have learned)

Now tell him that you are going to count slowly, and that as you say each number you wish him to close his eyes, then to open them, and be ready to close them again by the time you say the next number. For instance, you slowly count, "One, two, three, four." At each count, the subject is to close his eyes and open them in-between-counts. He is to keep his eyes focused on yours throughout the process, even when they are closed.

Start counting now slowly and in rhythm, and you will find that as you continue the counting that the period during which the subject's eyes remain open becomes shorter and shorter, and finally instead of the eyes opening there will only be a movement of the eyebrows while the lids remain closed. See Fig. 19.

Many subjects will go into hypnosis via this method by the time you have counted to only fifteen or twenty, and it is rarely necessary to count over one hundred.

When you find the eyes are closed and the subject does not seem able to open them, instead of continuing with the counting begin to say, in exactly the same rhythm and tone as your previous counting, "Sleep. Sleep. Sleepy, Sleepy. Sleep. You -- are -- going -- to -- sleep. Fast -- fast -- asleep. Asleep. Sleep.

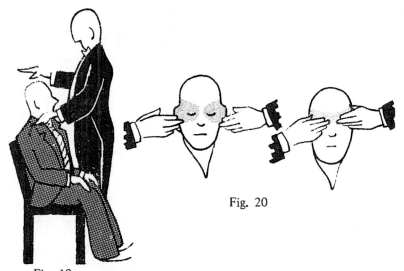

Fig. 20

Fig. 19

Sleepy. Sleep, etc."

Soon the subject's head will drop forward, and you will notice he is very drowsy. At this point, you can commence some of the head stroking passes, as previously explained, while you suggest "the sleep formula" to your subject until hypnosis is achieved.

2. The Bill Baras Method:

In this rather unusual technique the subject is comfortably seated in front of a bright light which shines directly into his eyes. To spare him from the light, he is requested to close his eyes. Use a bright light and place it at such a level that the subject has to look up towards it. This will necessitate his leaning his head back so that the muscles of the neck will be drawn tight and taught.

Next, hold your hand in front of the subject's closed eyes, about two inches from his face, casting a heavy shadow over them. This shadow is held for a short time, and is suddenly removed. The effect of this is to bring to the closed eyes a sensation of darkness that quickly changes to diffused redness, as the light sifts into the closed eyes.

Again repeat the shadow effect, and again pull it suddenly away. By drawing your hands off to each side of the subject's face, the shadow will pass in that direction. By drawing the hands past the eyes in an upward direction, the shadow will follow accordingly. See Fig. 20.

Vary the process, but always keep the effect of shadow to light, shadow to light, shadow to light following a definite pattern in rhythm. Continue this process for about five minutes. With many subjects you will find this method to work very effectively.

You can learn more of the technique if you will experiment with it on yourself, as you observe that even though your eyelids are tightly shut, the light can still be plainly noted as a sort of reddish glare as it penetrates through the closed lids. When you work with a subject using this method you will find it convenient to stand behind him as he is seated in the chair, and bend your head in low so that you are breathing directly upon either the top of his head or upper forehead, as shown in Fig. 21.

Now, in this method very little verbal suggestion need be used. As you proceed with the technique keep your gaze fixed on the top of the subject's head, and concentrate (to yourself) on the subject getting drowsy, and finally that he is going soundly to sleep. Whatever the stages in the induction of hypnosis you wish to develop in your subject such as relaxation, heaviness of limbs, drowsiness, sleep, etc. think of these mentally to yourself. In other words, *give your suggestions mentally to your subject;* give your suggestions to your subject just as you would verbally, but don't speak them -- THINK THEM!

Follow on in this method by making very gentle passes over the face of the subject. For most part these passes are made without contact, about two inches distant from the surface of the skin, only occasionally do you allow your fingers to touch his cheeks lightly here and there.

Then rub the forehead softly, and continue on with more of the noncontact passes in front of his face casting the shadows. Sometimes open your fingers as you pass them between the light and his closed eyes; this produces a flickering effect. This flickering shadow is very hypnotic. Then again close your fingers and make the shadow solid and dark. Sometimes use just one hand in making the shadow, and sometimes both. Make passes now without contact over the body of the subject going from his face as far down as the stomach. Then make passes down over his shoulders and chest, sometimes touching lightly, and sometimes without contact.

As you continue with this process, you will notice the subject will develop a marked quivering of the eyelids, and his head will frequently fall forward on his chest; you can assist this by gently pushing his head forwards. The muscles of his mouth will also seem to become somewhat drawn, and his breathing will deepen.

Your subject's head having fallen forward and his breathing having become deep and regular, turn out the light, and softly, so softly that your voice is barely a whisper, commence giving "the sleep formula" of verbal suggestions. As you give these suggestions make short passes with contact down the arms, and

This method will be found very useful in working with nervous persons; it is not tiring to the subject and is very soothing. Being highly esthetic, it can be especially recommended for hypnotizing women.

3. The Gil Boyne Method:

Gil Boyne is one of the most creative hypnotists in America. The method to be described, which he referred to as his "Rock-a-bye method," is his favorite technique for rapidly hypnotizing a solo subject.

Have the subject stand facing you, and ask him to look into your eyes as you fasten your gaze on the root of his nose. Then place your hands on his shoulders, and in a tone of positive authority say, "I am going to put you deeply asleep. I want you to relax. Your body will grow very light; you can feel it! You must feel it for you are going to sleep. You are going to sleep! Deep asleep!"

Now begin to rock the subject's body gently to and from you; do this rocking action in a slow, easy manner See Fig. 22.

Continue your positive barrage of suggestions that he is going to sleep! That his eyelids are heavy and will close! Then command forcefully, "Close your eyes!"

Next, place your fingers over his closed eyes, while you continue gently rocking his body, repeat, "Deep asleep! You are going deep asleep! Sleep deep now! GO SOUND ASLEEP!"

Gill Boyne is a large man of forceful demeanor. His method embodies an affirmative approach in the giving of suggestions, and illustrates how the method of hypnotizing one employs may be created

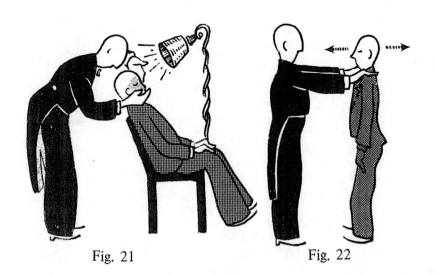

Fig. 21   Fig. 22

to fit your particular personality. Most frequently the persuasive approach to hypnotizing is used, however there are times when an aggressive approach works very well. Psychologically speaking, one might say that there are two types of hypnotists: (1) *the mother type* who comforts and consoles the subject via the protective instinct, and (2) *the father type* who is the master of the situation and operates via the authoritative response; as to which approach is best it is difficult to say. It rather depends upon the personality of the subject with which one is working, and some hypnotists are sensitive enough to size up the individual and apply either a persuasive or authoritative technique as seem most applicable to the particular case.

Psychologist, R . W . White sums the matter of hypnotic responsiveness by the subject in this theory, "Hypnotic behavior should be regarded as meaningful, goal-directed striving, its most general goal being behave like a hypnotized person as this is continually defined by the operator and understood by the subject."

4. The Ormond McGill Method:

For most general practice this method will be found highly effective. It offers something of an innovation in hypnotic technique.

Have your subject take a seat in a comfortable chair and relax back. Take a position about two feet in front of him and request that he look directly into *your right eye,* indicating the eye into which he is to stare with a gesture of your hand. You, in turn, stare back at him focusing your gaze directly upon *his right eye.* Tell him not to gaze wander under any conditions, and to con centrate intently upon every thought you give him. See. Fig. 23

You will note that this *right eye to right eye* handling is a variation of "the hypnotic gaze" which you gave learned. It is effective as it maintains a one point focus while allowing you the opportunity to observe that the attention of the subject is unwavering.

Now, the underlying secret that makes this method unique and so productive of positive results is that, in its process, *the operator mildly hypnotizes himself as he entrances his subject.* Thus he feels and experiences the same sensations which his subject is experiencing, and since the method employs a progressive series of hypnotic suggestions that takes the subject along, sensation by sensation, through the various stages of relaxation on down to deep hypnosis, the operator is enabled to *time* the giving of the proper suggestions.

Secondly, this process tends to place the hypnotist and the subject enrapport with each other. As the hypnotist presents each suggestion series to the subject, *he firmly concentrates upon same, in his own mind visualizing that he is projecting the sensation-ideas mentally right along with the suggestive-words verbally to his subject.* Since the operator is experiencing the same sensations induced by the suggestions himself, this is readily done.

In actual practice, the process works like this by way of example:

In the course of your suggestion series, let us say, you have come to the point where the eyes are becomming heavy and fatigued. You experience the sensation of tiredness in your own eyes, so you know that when you give the suggestions, "Your eyes are heavy and tired. They are so tired they smart. How badly you want to close them You simply must close them." that your subject is experiencing exactly the same sensations, thus the physical reactions of the subject tie-in with the suggestions. *Each reenforce the other.*

And, as you present the suggestions, not only do you say the words, but, at the same time, you concentrate your mind on the idea of your subject's eyes being thus heavy and tired and wanting to close. *Do this by visualizing a mental-picture of his eyes becoming so fatigued.* In this manner, step by step, you mentally visualize your verbal suggestions as you apply this method. With this understanding of the introspective aspects of the process, your subject seated comfortably relaxed before you staring into your eye as you stare back into his, you are ready to proceed.

Suggest to the subject, "As you look into my eye, you will begin to feel a most pleasant calm creeping over you as you relax all of the muscles in your body. Relax the muscles of your head and face, right on down through the muscles of your neck and shoulders. Every muscle relaxing throughout your entire body, right on down to your feet. You are becomming so relaxed and calm. All is so quiet and calm. It is just like a heavy, dark cloak being draped about and over your body. All is so quiet and calm."

As you give your suggestions, make short slow passes downward in the direction of your subject. Perform these in a sort of downward ellipse, starting with both hands in near your face, then bringing the hands out and downward towards your subject, and completing the elongated circle by bringing your hands back again towards your face. See Fig. 24.

Make these passes rather unobtrusive, more to emphasize your subject's attention to your eye and suggestions than to cause notice of themselves.

Proceed with your suggestions, "... and your eyes are getting fixed, set upon mine." As you say this, make a gesture directly from his right eye to yours. "And how tired your eyes are

Fig. 24

Fig. 23

becoming. The lids are getting so heavy that they just want to blink and close. How you want to close those tired eyes. But, they won't close yet because they are set, looking directly into my eye. How your eyes burn and smart. How you want to close them, they are so heavy, so tired. How badly you want to close them. All right, let them close and get relief. I will count slowly from one to ten. With every count your eyes will get heavier and heavier, until by the time I reach 'ten,' or before, they will be tightly closed. Ready now ... one, two ... your eyes are getting so very, very heavy, they are beginning to close. Three. How heavy your eyelids are, you can hardly keep them open a moment longer. Your eyes are closing. Four, five. Let your tired eyes close now. That's it, they are so heavy and tired. Close your eyes now. Six. Seven. That's it, close those tired tired eyes. Eight. Nine. TEN! Eyes closed All down tight together now shutting out the light. Eyes closed tight!"

Time the giving of these suggestions to the manner in which your own eyes feel, and also time them to the reactions of your subject as you observe his eyelids wink, blink, and droop. By the time you reach the count of "ten, his eyes should be tightly closed. If they are not, then gently close the lids with your fingertips as you suggest, "Close those tired eyes now, and let them rest."

Then continue:

"How good it feels to close those tired eyes. They are so tired, it feels so good to rest them. They are shut tightly, and are shutting tighter and tighter. So tight that they are getting stuck together. They are stuck so tightly they will not open anymore. They are stuck shut together... stuck tight!"

Place your right thumb in the center of your subject's forehead at this point and push downwards towards the root of his

49

nose, while gripping, at the same time, his right wrist in your left hand. Further suggest, "You cannot open your eyes now no matter how hard you try. They are fastened tightly together, see how they stick. Try and open them, but you cannot!"

Your subject will try in vain to open his eyes; his eyebrows will rise and fall, but the lids will remain stuck together. After the subject has tried to open his eyes for a few seconds, continue:

"Its all right, just forget all about your eyes ... just let them rest ... and let yourself rest ... and go to sleep now. Just rest and go sound asleep. Sound, sound asleep. Your eyes are resting and you are resting, and you are going sound asleep. So sound asleep. Sleep!"

Now step behind your subject and gently make stroking passes over his forehead from the center outward towards the temples, as shown in Fig. 25.

Continue this stroking action as you suggest, "Everything is becoming quiet and calm. You are so quiet and calm. You are getting drowsy and sleepy. Go sound asleep. Everything is fading away. You are going to sleep; down deep asleep. Down, down, deep asleep. Things are all getting farther and farther away, even my voice is getting farther away, and as it gets more and more distant you are sinking down deeper and deeper to sleep."

At this point, lower your voice and speak softer and softer accompaning these suggestions of your voice getting farther away. Then gradually resume you normal tone for these suggestions, "You are going down deep asleep. Sleepy sleep. Sound, sound asleep. Sleep deep. Your muscles are all relaxed. Your head is getting heavy, it is falling forward on your chest."

Gently give the subject's head a little push so that it will fall forward, then begin stroking the back of his neck from the top part of his head down to the base of his brain. In this stroking process, locate the small depressed spot between the first and second vertebrae at the very top of the spinal column. Press in firmly upon this spot with the tip or side of your right forefinger. See Fig. 26. It produces a numbing sensation, as you suggest, "How numb everything feels. You are so drowsy and sleepy. Go sound asleep. Every muscle all over your body, from the very top of your head down to your feet, is relaxed and at rest."

Now place your hands in the center of your subject's shoulders (on each side) and press downward, as shown in Fig. 27. Slump his body down in his chair as much as possible, and suggest, "Your hands and arms are so heavy. So very, very heavy. You can feel them weighing heavily in your lap. And the fingers are beginning to tingle. And your legs, too, are getting so heavy. They are pressing heavier upon the floor, as you sink down deep and deeper to sleep.

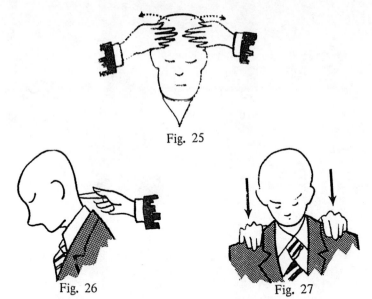

Fig. 25

Fig. 26   Fig. 27

"Now your breaths are beginning to deepen. Breathe deep and free. Breathe deep and free. Breathe deep and free."

Step back and observe your subject for a moment and note if the breathing is deepening; if so, it indicates that your suggestions are "taking hold." Next step in close and place your nose to your subject's ear and inhale and exhale forcefully. Watch the subject closely at this point, and note that he picks up the tempo of your breathing as his inhalations become deep and full. Suggest, "You are breathing deep and full. Deep and full. Suggest, "You are breathing deep and full. Deep and full. Deep and full, and every breath you take is sending you down deeper and deeper to sleep. Go sound asleep. Go sound asleep– down deep, deep asleep."

Move around to the front of your subject now and make long, slow downward passes from the top of his head to his lap. Make these close to the body, but without contact as shown in Fig. 28.

Suggest, "Sound, sound asleep. Sleep. See how limp and relaxed your arms are. They are limp just like rags."

Pick up one of the subject's hands from his lap and let it drop back, Then push his hands deliberately from his lap and they will fall limply to his sides, where they dangle rag-like.

Suggest, "Nothing bothers you in the slightest. Just sleep quietly and calmly. My voice seems very far away, and you are sleeping deeply and peacefully.

"Now when I press upon your fingernails, you will pass on down deeper into an even more profound sleep -- way down deep into the very deepest of hypnotic sleeps."

51

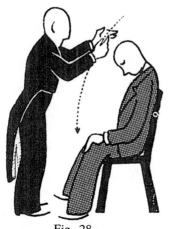

Fig. 28

Fig. 29

Pick up his hands and place them again in his lap, and press with your thumbs upon the roots of the nails of his second and third fingers, between the first knuckle joint and the nail. See Fig 29. Make the pressure firm and even as you suggest, "As I press on your fingers, you will go deeper and yet deeper to sleep. Way down D- E - E - P ASLEEP! WAY DOWN DEEP ASLEEP!"

Pick up your subject's hands, hold them out free from his lap and let them suddenly drop. If they fall limply, without resistance, dangling like rags, then suggest, "Now as you sleep nothing will disturb you, and you will follow every suggestion I present to you. Nothing will bother or disturb you in the least, and you will continue going on down deeper and deeper to sleep in the hypnotic trance . . asleep in deep hypnosis."

I call my method of hypnotizing "the progressive approach" as the subject is led gradually from response to one series of suggested effects onto the next in a progressive manner, each suggestion-series leading on towards deeper hypnosis. Practice and master this method well as in its production you will learn a variety of subtleties that are hypnotic in effect; likewise it is important to your subsequent work in entertaining with hypnotism.

It would be possible to present many additional techniques for including hypnosis, but these along with "The Relaxation Method," in the next chapter, will be ample. As you proceed with your work you will soon develop your own style, techniques, and suggestions formulas.

The essential thing to bear in mind in the development of any hypnotic technique is that your method must capture and hold your subject's attention while you drive home suggestions that will be uncritically accepted. To such ends, *remove as much outside stimuli as possible from the subject as this will narrow*

52

and focus his attention field which is important to the induction of hypnosis. In fact, it is in the deliberate controlling of outside stimuli that is the means of our entering the normal condition of sleep that we experience nightly. Consider:

At night we lie down and shut out the light. Our sense of sight becomes nil and that source of stimuli is removed. We lie quietly in bed and our sense of feeling and motion is restricted. The room is quiet and still, thus the auditory sense becomes lulled. Likewise, while in bed, our olfactory and taste senses are largely dormant. And sleep comes.

So it is in the induction of hypnosis, the state is produced just like natural sleep with the exception of one fundamental difference. In normal sleep all of the senses are dulled, while in hypnosis all of the senses are dulled with the exception of one, and that one is peaked.

You know how it is in cases of blind and/or deaf persons; when one or more of their senses are lost the others tend to compensate and develop to a hyper degree. In hypnosis, there is also this tendency, and it is through the avenue of this heightened (or peaked) sense that a rapport to the mind of the subject is maintained and suggestions may be implanted directly. The accompanying graphs clearly show the process.

In Graph A, we have a person in his normal waking state. Note how a variety of stimuli are entering his "Mind's Field of Attention," as I have termed it, in varying degrees of intensity. See Fig. 30.

In Graph B (see Fig. 31), we have a person in the process of being hypnotized. Note how the variety of stimuli have been leveled out, and one is strongly emphasized. It is through this heightened channel of contact to the mind that the suggestions are presented.

In actual hypnotic procedure, the subject is seated comfortably relaxed back in a chair and told to move as little as is possible, thus the stimuli of touch, smell and taste are reduced to a minimum. The eyes are next fatigued and shortly close; stimuli of sight has been removed. Only the sense of hearing remains, and, as above mentioned, *it is through this heightened channel of contact to the mind that the suggestions are given. Thus comes hypnosis.*

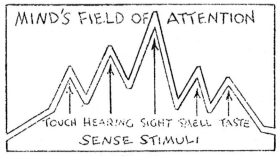

Fig. 30

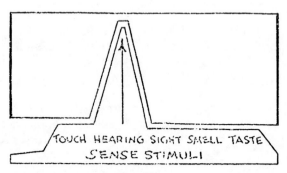

Fig. 31

7
The Relaxation Method
of Hypnotism

The Dave Elman Method:

I am devoting a special chapter to this technique of hypnotizing as not only is it an excellent method but also provides a good consideration of certain principles basic to successful induction. This method is especially interesting as it is applied without presenting suggestions of sleep. In fact, very little reference is made to hypnotism, the subject's attention being directed toward relaxation, and yet a deep hypnosis is induced.

First, consider these two important concepts:

1. Consent. The consent of the subject (willingness) to be hypnotized is basic to the successful induction of hypnosis. This can be either a conscious acceptance or an unconscious acceptance, that can be summed up in the word, *expectancy,.* In relation to hypnosis, such being the expectancy of being hypnotized.

2. Communication. There must be an avenue of communication between the operator and the subject. American hypnotist, Arnold Furst, in his work in Japan, has on occasion successfully hypnotized Japanese subjects who did not understand a word of English. If an understanding of the expected hypnotic occurrence can be conveyed to the subject, either through an interpreter or by the subject watching other persons hypnotized, the hypnotizing technique can be successful even in pantomine. For really practical application however, it is best that both the hypnotist and the subject think and speak in the same language.

In performing this method of hypnotizing, invite the subject to try the experience by stating, "I will show you a wonderful way of being hypnotized that will make you feel wonderful. This method is often used by doctors to relieve tension. In fact, a physician probably would not even refer to it as hypnotism, but would define it as being concentrated relaxation of mind and body. It will relax you and make you feel fine. Would you like to try the experience?"

Obtain the subject's verbal consent. Now present this pattern of suggestions:

"Fine then. Please seat yourself in this comfortable chair and relax. Let me take your hand for just a moment. Now, relax the hand I am holding as much as you can. Relax it so it becomes completely loose and limp. That's excellent."

By noting the subject's response in relaxing his hand as it rests in yours, you can immediately determine his state of mind in relation to following your suggestions. Insist on his achieving complete relaxation. When his hand is relaxed as it should be, you proceed on.

"Now take a long, deep breath. Hold it a moment, now let it out slowly. Once more take a deep breath, hold it, now let it out. It relaxes you.

"Now let your eyes close to get rid of all tension. Feels better already, doesn't it! Now relax the muscles around your eyes; relax them so completely that they feel loose and limp, and when you are sure they are so relaxed that the muscles won't work, try to make them work. If they are really relaxed as they should be, they won't work at all. You will find that you cannot open your eyes at all because the muscles of your eyes are so relaxed. That is real deep relaxation."

At this point in the induction process, the subject has by-passed his "sense of judgement," which is his conscious mind telling him that he can close and open his eyes at will. If he should open his eyes, tell him that he has just proved that he has not completely relaxed his eye muscles as yet, as they still operate. Request him to concentrate further on the relaxation of those muscles so they become so completely relaxed that they do not work. Have him test his eyes, and if they remain closed proceed with these further suggestions:

"Now that your eyes are closed and the muscles of your eyes are completely relaxed, you will find that you can relax much deeper than ever, and you feel wonderful. Now just extend that same feeling of complete relaxation right down through your entire body, on down to the very tips of your toes. Isn't that a nice feeling!

"Now here is something very interesting. When I ask you to, I want you to gently open and close your eyes. You can do this, and you will find that you will be able to relax *ten times* as much as you are right now. All the other muscles of your body will continue being completely relaxed, only your eyes will open and close gently when I tell them to. All ready, one . two ..three .. open your eyes gently . . now close them . . and relax *ten times* as much as your were before. Notice that surge of relaxation this brings over you. Now, when you do that again, just *double* your relaxation this time, and you will feel like you have a blanket of relaxation covering you from head to foot. Ready again . . . one, two, three, now open your eyes and now close them, and *double* the relaxation you had, and you will feel that blanket of relaxation covering you from head to foot."

Throughout this initial procedure, you have been holding the subject's relaxed hand in yours. Follow with these suggestions:

"Now, when I drop your hand, it will fall just like a limp rag into your lap, and you will be completely relaxed."

Release his hand and let it fall like a rag into his lap. You have induced hypnosis. You are now ready to deepen the state by this excellent technique. Suggest to the subject:

"You have achieved a splendid state of physical relaxation, but if you can relax mentally as well, you will find it will make you feel a hundred times as good as you do right now. Here is how you can do it. When I tell you to, I want you to start counting backward, beginning with the number one hundred, and each time you say a number, *double your relaxation,* and by the time you get to number ninety-seven, the numbers will have been relaxed right out of your mind. They will simply fade and disappear, and you will not be able to find any more numbers. Now, relax deeply, say that first number, *double your relaxation,* and watch what happens."

Subject says the first number, "One Hundred." *You remark:*

"That's fine. Double your relaxation now and the numbers will fade away. Say the second number now."

Subject says, "Nine-nine." *You remark:*

"Now double your relaxation again, and all the numbers disappear. Say only one more number, and they'll all be gone."

Subject says, "Ninety-eight." *You remark:*

Now all the numbers will be gone! All gone! You can't see any more numbers. That's fine. Now relax more with every breath you take, and notice how wonderful you feel!

If the subject continues to count on backward from one hundred at this point, stop him with the suggestion: "You are doing fine, but stop saying any more numbers. Relax in between the numbers. Only relaxation will make them disappear." *If the subject seems to be losing the numbers, then state,* "Now, I will pick up your right hand and drop it into your lap, and as I drop it let those numbers drop right out of your mind at the same time." *Drop his hand limply into his lap, and suggest:* "There, the numbers are all gone. The numbers have dropped right out of your mind. They are all gone and you can't find any more numbers. The numbers are all gone from your mind, and your mind as well as your body is relaxed now."

This process has placed the subject in a condition of hypnotic somnambulism (deep hypnosis), and has started the commencement of amnesia as exemplified in the forgotten number sequence. Note that you have not stated he could not remember any numbers you have stated that he cannot find any. This explicit use of language is the key to effective suggestion. Continue the induction process further by testing for increased amnesia, as you suggest:

"Now you are relaxed so completely both physically and mentally, that if I asked your phone number you wouldn't be able to find it to tell me . . would you?"

Subject responds with a shake of his head or a whispered. "No." You have induced hypnosis with an amnesia response in this gentle way, and you can proceed on to other hypnotic experiments from this point.

As I commented in the first paragraph of this chapter, it will be noted that in this method of hypnotism no mention or suggestion of sleep is given. The entire attention of the subject is centered on the idea of achieving physical and mental relaxation. Hypnosis can be induced very effectively this way.

Here are some observations you will make when you apply this method of hypnotizing:

As the subject goes into hypnosis, you will note a fluttering of the eyelids; a development of body warmth; a light tearing of the eyes; an upward roll of the eyes into the head as the eye muscles relax; an increasing of the pulse rate.

If the hands are warm and slightly moist, it indicates that the subject is responding splendidly. If the hands are warm but damp, it indicates the subject is doing well but is nervous. If the hands remain cold and dry, it indicates that the subject is resisting the suggestions, and that more explanation of how he is to relax and concentrate is desirable.

Now here is an important process for deepening hypnosis which is called, *compounding of suggestions.* As this is something the student should well understand, I will describe an experiment using such in action, viz.:

You have hypnotized a person, and present a posthypnotic suggestion such as this, "When I have you open your eyes, you will feel fine, but when you see me touch my necktie, you will have an irresistible urge to rise from your chair, walk over to the table and turn on the radio. You will then return to your chair, and close your eyes again. Open your eyes now and follow those suggestions."

After a moment of capturing the subject's attention, you touch your necktie. If the subject is very responsive, on this "cue," he will rise from his chair, go over to the table and turn on the radio, and will then return to his chair, close his eyes, exactly as you suggested he would do.

However, it may be that the subject, on seeing the hypnotic "cue" of the operator touching his tie, will not at first respond completely but merely turns and looks towards the radio. So you proceed to touch your tie again, and this time the subject more keenly glances at the radio, and possibly rises from his chair. For a third time you touch you necktie, and the subject moves over to the table, turns on the radio, and then returns to his chair completing the series of suggestions.

This is what is meant by the *compounding of suggestion,* i.e., each time the hypnotic "cue" (in this case the touching of your necktie) is given by the hypnotist, the original suggestion is made stronger, until the subject cannot disregard it. It builds in strength to become a compulsion.

Here is another example of the *compounding of suggestion* in operation:

The subject, after being hypnotized, is told that his arm is so stiff that he cannot move it no matter how hard he tries. When he tries and is unsuccessful, the hypnotist says, "Now, when I snap my fingers, you will be able to lower your arm and go much deeper to sleep in hypnosis." The hypnotist snaps his fingers, and the subject's arm falls to his lap. This is *compounding of suggestions:* the one suggestion (as the arm falls) causing the second suggestion (go deeper to sleep in hypnosis) to build into effect. Each suggestion compliments and compounds the other, and the operation of each increases the power of both.

You will note that this *compounding of suggestion* principle was used in "The Relaxation Method of Hypnotizing" technique, previously described, in the giving to the subject the suggestion that when he opens his eyes and then closes them that he will relax ten times as much, and then that when he again opens and closes them, that he will double the relaxed state he was in prior to that occurrence. The subconscious mind is great for logic, and this mathematical implication of increased strength by multiplied ratio carries great power. Thus, when you have a state of relaxation commenced in the subject, you compound it into a deeper state.

Compounding of suggestion is an effective process to use on all suggestions provided the suggestions are ones that the subject will accept, and its usefulness does not apply only to deepening of hypnosis, but is helpful to the acceptance and effectiveness of all suggestions, as illustrated in this hypothetical physician/hypnotist/patient experience of removing a nervous tension headache by the technique.

The physician in the handling does not tell the patient that he does not have a headache, but rather that as the subject relaxes more and more (the suggestion is compounded) that he will feel better and better, and that which bothered him before doesn't bother him now.

There are likewise, other principles in the correct handling of suggestion to be found in the example above, i.e., in the noting that the naming of the discomfort is omitted from the suggestions, and no exaggerated claims are made such as that the patient will never again have a headache. These are important principles for the student to appreciate as direct naming of a discomfort, when the subject is in a suggestible condition, tends to call attention to the discomfort exaggerated claims tend to arouse the critical faculties of the subject which results in direct ratio to a lessening of the power of the suggestion.

The correct handling in this therapy session example continues, "Now that you are completely relaxed and that which bothered you a while ago doesn't bother you now, notice how good you feel. I am sure that with a little instruction in relaxation you will be able to handle the tension if it occurs again, and eventually you won't be bothered with it at all. "

The subject is now told to open his eyes, and the suggestion is quickly given, "All gone isn't it!" The statement is made as a positive affirmation, not as a question. The patient will answer in the affirmative. *The headache is gone!*

I have gone to some length going over these principles of properly giving suggestions as they reemphasize what you have already learned, and are important to your hypnotic training. They are universal in application to all hypnotic phenomena.

8
The Phenomena
of Hypnosis

Having hypnotized your subject, what has happened? You observe him seated relaxed in the chair, possibly with his head drooped forward on his chest, breathing heavily and looking very much as if he had dozed off for a nap. Indeed, left to himself he would pass from the hypnotic condition, in which you have placed him, into normal sleep, and would awaken awhile later of his own accord.

However, at the moment, despite outward appearances, your subject is not asleep in the accepted sense of that state. He is hypnotized, and while in that unique condition is willing to accept and automatically act upon suggestions from you uncritically. Your suggestions are capable of producing in the subject some most unusual and interesting phenomena characteristic of the hypnotic condition, i.e., muscular catalepsies, somnambulistic effects similar to "sleep walking," illusions, hallucinations, and posthypnotic effects. Let us observe each of these phenomena in operation with a few experiments.

First, let's try a simple experiment in muscular catalepsy. Such tests are designed to cause the subject's muscles to set in a suggested manner so they will not respond to his "will" for the moment. In this instance, tell your hypnotized subject that his muscles are so set that he cannot get out of his chair. His legs are so stiff and rigid in the sitting position that he cannot rise from the chair no matter how hard he tries.

In responding to this suggestion, the subject will strive to rise from his chair but finds himself unable to do so. He will pull and struggle, his muscles seem to have become cataleptic and are incapable of lifting his body from the chair.

Then snap your fingers beside his ear and tell him to relax again, that the influence is all gone, and that he can now rise easily from his chair. The subject is immediately able to stand.

With the subject standing, you can reserve the experiment and tell him that his body is so stiff and rigid that this time he will find that he is unable to seat himself. The subject ackwardly tries to take a seat but is totally unable to do so, until you remove the influence with the suggestion, "All right now .. your muscles are all relaxed once again, you feel fine. Go ahead and be seated."

The response to such suggestions by the hypnotized subject (incidentally, a person in hypnosis is technically referred to as a *hypnotic,* which term we will henceforth frequently use in this text) are so forceful that one may well wonder if some caution should not be used. Assuredly yes! While the state of hypnosis is not dangerous in itself, as it is one of both mental and physical relaxation, it does render the hypnotic hyper-responsive to suggestion. Accordingly, it is obvious that care must be used in regard to what specific suggestions are given the subject, as their influence is strong. Make it your rule that suggestions which are disturbing should never be given. As an entertainer with hypnotism, only present suggestions which are pleasant and interesting; the reaction to such suggestions will then always be enjoyable. Also, remember this important principle in relation to the correct manner of giving hypnotic suggestions:

Having completed one suggestion-series, before ever presenting a new set of suggestion-series, always remove completely the influence of the first set before the second is commenced, by telling the hypnotic to forget what you have just said, to relax and sleep on deeply for a few moments before he tries anything else.

This is a vital point to keep in mind for the correct handling of the hypnotic state, otherwise one set of suggestions might conflict with another.

By way of an example, imagine what would occur if you told a hypnotic that he was unable to rise from his chair, and while he was trying in vain to do so, you suddenly suggested that he would feel an irressible impulse to rise at once.

What happens?

In most cases, the stronger of the two impulses (as induced by the suggestions) would dominate, and the subject would react accordingly. But, in the case of a very sensitive person, these two opposing suggestions - - working simultaneously in opposite directions - - might develop a neurotic conflict which would be very disturbing to the subject resulting in hysterical actions such as tears, etc. *So, in your experimenting make it a consciencious rule to give only one series of suggestions at a time, and always remove their effects totally from the subject before going on to anotner experiment.*

As a student of hypnotism, please reread this rule again as it must be always with you in the performance of the hypnotic art.

Here is another experiment in muscular catalepsy which you can try as you observe the phenomena of hypnosis:

Take your subject's arm and raise it out at a right angle from his body, suggesting that it is becoming stiff and rigid like a bar of steel. You will immediately feel the muscles of the arm tighten, and the arm will remain rigidly outstretched.

Now suggest that the arm is so stiff that he cannot bend it no matter how hard he tries. The subject will try as hard as he can but is unable to bend it. Then suggest that at the count of "three his arm will instantly relax, will fall limply to his side, and as it drops to his side it will send him down deeper to sleep in hypnosis.

Count, "One, two, three!" and the subject's arm relaxes and drops to his side.

You can fairly well judge by the way that arm falls just how deeply in hypnosis your subject is. If the arm instantly collapses on cue and falls limp like a rag to his side, you can be more or less certain he is entranced. On the other hand, if he lowers his arm slowly, as though under voluntary control, it is a good indication that he is not as yet deeply affected and it is well to continue your hypnotizing process longer before proceeding on to further experiments.

In watching your subject's arm drop instantly from a cataleptic condition to complete relaxation, you are observing in action an example of the excellent relaxation which hypnosis brings to the body. Likewise, note the bit of technique you have employed in using the response to a suggested action to deepen the entire state, as emphasized in the suggestion, ".. 'as his arm relaxes and falls limply to his side it will send him down yet deeper to sleep in hypnosis." This technique is, of course, the "compounding of suggestions" principle we have carefully studied, via which the response to one suggestions (or suggestion series) increases the overal pattern of suggestibility in the subject.

You can now try for a somnambulistic response, as you suggest to the hypnotic that he will stand up from his chair, and as he does so, he will continue to sink down even yet deeper to sleep in hypnosis. (Here again note the "compounding" technique in giving suggestions) Command him to arise and then to walk, and you will be observing a condition similar to "sleep walking." In truth, you have induced the somnambulistic state.

You will note how simple and direct are the suggestions given the subject while he is in the hypnotic state to enlisit responses. Lone repetitions of suggestions are not necessary to produce reactions in hypnosis, as the subject is so suggestible in the condition that only the bare essentials of the idea need be given to cause the action. In fact, some subjects are so alert to suggestions while in trance that they will almost seem to pick up subliminal cues to the suggested action from the operator even before such have been given verbally.

Tell the hypnotic to return to his chair, to relax back in it, and to continue going down deeper, deeper to sleep. You are now ready to experiment with an illusion.

An illusion, or false impression of an object, always requires a tangible article of some sort as the initial stimulus around which the illusion develops. In this case, for the center of the stimulus, you hand the subject a broom and suggest that in a moment he will open his eyes and will see in his arms a beautiful girl, his girl friend. Then suggest when you tell him to that he will open his eyes and look at the girl, and will kiss her enthusiastically. Further suggest that when he opens his eyes and see this girl it will send him down even deeper asleep in the hypnotic trance (compounding of suggestions again).

Command the subject to open his eyes. On seeing the broom in his arms he instantly interprets it as his girl friend, and gives the broom a kiss.

On paper this stunt sounds rather on the foolish side, but in performance it is extremely amusing. Such "foolish" stunts have an occasional use in providing the lighter moments of the hypnotic entertainment. It must be born in mind that in volunteering to be hypnotized at an entertainment the subject accepts the situation in the spirit of fun and reacts accordingly. However, it is well that the performer be sufficient of a psychologist to judge his subjects correctly, as you certainly do not wish to embarrass anyone. Most people who volunteer to participate in a show have sufficient exhibitionistic natures to enjoy it thoroughly, but there are sometimes people who are sensitive. So be careful when you present stunts of this kind, and use such only on subjects who obviously appreciate good natured feats. After all, you are dealing with fellow human beings who have voluntarily placed themselves in your hands for the expressed purpose of conducting hypnotic experiments. This implies a confidence in you, *and as a hypnotist, you must always respect that confidence.*

By and large, make it your rule as a stage hypnotist never to attempt any demonstration on anyone else that you wouldn't be perfectly willing to have performed on yourself. *And use good taste.*

Now suggest to your subject that his dream girl (the broom) is fading away, that his eyes are again closing, and that he is going back to sleep. Gently take the broom away from him, and you are ready to experiment with an hallucination.

An hallucination is similar to an illusion in that it conjures up an imaginary impression (or sensation), but in the production of such it makes use of no material cue for the development of the illusion. In other words, an hallucination develops purely on the strength of your suggestions alone.

Tell your subject that he is now sleeping deeply, but that when you count to "three" he will open his eyes, will look at his left hand, and will see in it the cutest little canary bird he ever saw. Tell him that he will love this little bird, will play with it, and will watch it fly about the room.

The suggestions established, count to "three." The subject

opens his eyes, stares at his left hand, and goes through all the responses of playing with the little bird.

Does the hypnotic actually see the canary? It is only imaginary of course, but as an hallucination the experience is absolutely real to the subject as a hypnotic experience; a deeply influenced subject, at the time, actually believes the bird is really there. He sees and feels it. The phenomena is remarkable, and the resulting pantomine is truly amazing to witness.

Finally, when the experiment has proceeded sufficiently, suggest that the bird is fading away like a dream, that he is getting sleepy again, that his eyes are reclosing, and that he is sound asleep.

From this experiment you can go directly into a posthypnotic demonstration.

Suggest to your subject that in a moment you are going to awaken him, and that when he awakes he will feel fine and perfectly normal in all respects except that he will find that he is stuck to the seat of his chair, and will be entirely unable to rise no matter how hard he tries. Also tell him that he will remain stuck to the seat of the chair in this manner, and be unable to rise from it until such time that you snap your fingers by his ear and tell him that he can.

Now carefully awaken your subject from hypnosis by the method to be described in chapter nine, and casually ask him to get up from his chair. To his surprise, he will find that he cannot do so. He will struggle and tug but he seems stuck tight to his seat until such time as you snap your fingers by his ear and say, "All right, you can get up now, the influence is all gone!"

You may make an interesting observation here of hypnotic effects if you wish, by explaining to your subject, as he tries vainly to get up from his seat, that the only "force" is holding him stuck are your suggestions that he would be unable to rise presented while he was in hypnosis. Sometimes that realization enables him to break the posthypnotic effect, but often, even with such understanding, he is still unable to shake off the influence, until you give the cue to remove the suggestion. You have in this experimental manner illustrated how close to learned habits posthypnotic suggestions truly are.

Posthypnotic effects among the most interesting in the entire field of hypnotism, and are unquestionably the most important of all to therapy. For, if hypnotic influence only lasted while the subject was in the hypnotic state its use would be extremely limited, but through posthypnotic suggestions the effects can carry over into our daily lives. Many people seem puzzled as to how a hypnotic suggestion can continue on after the condition of hypnosis is removed. However, when we regard hypnotism as a state of mind in which ideas can be powerfully implanted in our nervous system, posthypnotic phenomena becomes the expected occurrence, just as any idea throughly learned becomes a continued part of our personality long after the original teacher has departed.

In this chapter, you have been taken rapidly through a series of experiments which illustrate well some of the major types of phenomena that may be produced in hypnosis.

In experimenting with your subject, it unlikely that you will wish to try to produce all of these phenomena at one session. Indeed, unless you have an exceptionally responsive subject, it would hardly be possible to obtain such a variety of effects. The experiments have been presented proceeding from the most easily achieved to the more difficult. You see, many subjects are able to respond to muscular catalepsy suggestions who are utterly unable to experience an hallucination, while some who experience an hallucination will fail to react to a posthypnotic. People all differ, and this diversity of results is to be expected.

In general, when experimenting with the phenomena of hypnosis follow approximately the order of these tests, working up through catalepsy, somnambulistic walking, illusions, hallucinations, to posthypnotic reactions.

Of last consideration to the phenomena of hypnosis arises the question, does the hypnotic remember what occurs to him after he awakens from the trance? I have mentioned this before; the answer is sometimes *yes* and sometimes *no*. Again we have the factor of subject differences at work, people vary in their reponses. Memory of hypnosis experience is much like the memory of dream experience. Sometimes they are buried so deeply there is no recall, in other instances the memory is hazy and indistinct and quickly fades, while others may be vivid enough to be complete. If there is any particular reason for wishing that amnesia be produced, the hypnotist can usually produce it by suggesting to that effect. It then occurs as a posthypnotic experience, as we have previously considered.

9
Experiments in the Hypnotic State

Now that you have learned how to hypnotize, and have practiced producing some of the fundamental phenomena of hypnosis, there lies before you a multitute of interesting experiments you can try. In this regard, it may be well to remention that in the presenting of suggestions to the hypnotized subject (the hypnotic) to produce these effects, your approach should be one of direction rather than persuasion. *In other words, tell the hypnotic clearly what he is expected to do:* the field of his attention is so concentrated in hypnosis that commands are instantly received, followed, and interpreted.

As an example, in stiffening the arm of the hypnotic, you do not say, "Please hold up your arm. Now think of it becoming stiff. You can feel it getting rigid and tense," as you would in prehypnotic tests. Rather you would say forcefully, "Raise your arm out straight. Your arm is stiff and rigid! You cannot bend it! Try hard to bend your arm but it is impossible!"

To reemphasize, in presenting suggestions to the hypnotic, make all of your suggestions directly to the point so as to be easily understood by the subject, and tell him exactly what he is to do.

Here is another example of this handling in relation to producing an hallucination, say as in establishing "a fishing scene:"

You commence by creating a "lake" in front of the subject. Tell him *exactly* what he is going to see when he opens his eyes, thus, "When you open your eyes, you will see before you a beautiful blue lake. You will enjoy seeing this lake very much. All right, sit up in your chair and get ready to see the lake. I will count three, and at the count of 'three' you will open your eyes, and will clearly see spread before you this beautiful blue lake. It will be a delight. And, as you look upon this lake it will send you continually down deeper and deeper asleep in the hypnotic trance."

There are some important bits of hypnotic technique given here it is well for you to learn, i.e. in the setting of the hallucination to occur on a given cue, in this case the opening of the eyes. and in the suggesting that witnessing the hallucination will deepen the sleep (trance). This is "compounding of suggestions" again and is important as possibly the opening of the eyes and the surprise of seeing the hallucination might snap the subject out of the trance.

Then count, "One, two, three." The subject opens his eyes, and goes through all of the pantomine of observing a beautiful lake. See. Fig. 32.

Fig. 32

You can now lead your subject through various aspects of the scene by handling him a stick, telling him it is a fishing pole, and that he is going fishing in the lake. If he is a person with a lively imagination, such suggestion will be sufficient, and he will portray the entire scene on his own initiative; baiting the hook, throwing the line in the lake, reeling in the fish, taking it off the hook, etc.

Conversely, if he is a more-or-less lethargic type of person, then you induce the various effect by step-by-step suggestions as, "Bait your hook. Now throw in your line into the lake and fish. That's it, you are fishing now. You just got a bite. Hook that fish. Reel him in, etc." The exact manner in which you handle any specific subject depends entirely upon the mental makeup of the individual which whom you are working. But, whatever your procedure to secure active hypnotic responses, the resulting pantomines are so true to life that you, right along with spectators, will be fascinated at the results.

Having completed "the fishing scene," tell him to close his eyes, to go back to sleep, that his fishing trip is now successfully completed, and that all he has to do is simply sleep. By this handling, the effects of the experiment are accordingly entirely removed, and you are then ready to perform another demonstration.

By way of examples of the effects you can produce, you can show the hypnotic roses where none exist, or you can make him think he is an orator or a singer by a simple suggestion. After the subject has been hypnotized, it is not necessary to rehypnotize the person for each illusion. One effect can be produced after the other during the same session in hypnosis. Indeed, if the effects are somewhat related to each other, the subject can be made to pass directly from each on to the next. *Always, however, remember to tell him to go to sleep and that the previous hypnotic effects are all gone before conducting a new type of an experiment of a conflicting nature.*

A Resume of Hypnotic Phenomena.

Here is a splendid consideration of various hypnotic experiments which may be performed with the hypnotic, with acknowledgement to the studies of Dr Bernard, viz.:

In response to your direct and specific suggestions, your subject may be rendered happy and elated, sad and dejected, angry or pleased, liberal or stingy, proud or humble, pugnacious or pacific, bold and timid, hopeful or despondent, insolent or respectful. He may be made to sing, to shout, to laugh, to weep, to act, to dance, to fish, to recite a beautiful poem, or to excogitate a profound argument.

The expression of your subject during these delusions is most important as its very earnestness is profound in its appeal. The attitudes and gestures are equal to, or surprassing, the best efforts of an accomplished actor, although the hypnotized subject may actually be a person of limited histrionics, and show no particular talent for mimicry in the waking state.

The hypnotized subject is not acting a part in the ordinary sense of the word. He *believes* himself to be the actual personality suggested. The subject will impersonate to perfection any suggested character with which he is familiar. Most effective tests can be performed by thus suggesting to the hypnotic that he is some popular movie or television star.

One of the most striking and important peculiarities of subconsciousness as distinguished from consciousness, consists in the prodigious memory of the former. In all degrees of hypnosis, this exaltation of the memory is one of the most pronounced of the attendant phenomena.

The remarkable effects of hypnotism in the recollection of circumstances and the revival of impression long since past is astonishing. Images which have been completely lost to ordinary memory and are not recoverable in the normal state of mind may be recalled. All the sensations which we have ever experienced have left behind them traces in the brain, so slight as to be untangible and imperceptible under ordinary circumstances, but hypnotic suggestion addressing itself to the subconscious side of the mind, within which is the storehouse of memories, can recall these memories at the command of the operator. Such recall of memories and experiences is technically known as "age regression." They have psychological value and belong to the field of the hypnotherapist.

Everything learned in normal life can be remembered in hypnosis, even when apparently it has long been forgotten.

Of course, false memories can also be suggested, as when you say to a subject, "You will remember the adventures we had on our trip to New York yesterday." and if it is al all plausible that we may have done so, the suggestion will take effect, and he will at once begin to relate all that be believes we did in New York. This is an example of a retroactive positive hallucination, because the subject believes that he has experienced something that really never occured. Also memories can be obliterated.

Sense delusions are likewise common in hypnotism; either as illusions or hallucinations. An illusion, you will recall, is the false interpretation of an existing external object, as, for instance, when a chair is taken for a horse, a broomstick for a beautiful woman, a noise in the street for orchestra music, or when you ask a subject if he would like to smoke, and he accepts a pencil in place of a cigarette and attempts to light it. That the illusion is real is evident by the fact that the subject will imagine he is drawing smoke from the pencil, which, of course, is not even lit, and will even cough if smoking is usually irritating to his throat.

Try these experiments with illusions: play on a real piano, then suggest that a table is a piano and play on that. Ask your subject which piano he likes better. He will scratch his head in deciding between them. Give your subject an empty glass and tell him it contains hot whiskey and water, and that he must take care not to burn his mouth. The ensuing endeavor to swallow the imaginary liquor is followed by catching of the breath and violent coughing.

As we have already discussed, an hallucination is the preception of an object which does not exist, as, for instance, when you say to your subject, "Sit down in this armchair." Where there is really no chair at all; yet the hallucination is so perfect that he does put himself in exactly the same attitude as if he were sitting in a real chair, only if you ask him after a time, "Are you comfortable?" he may reply, "Not particularly." and ask for a chair that is more to his liking. It seems increditable that an hallucination could be so real that a person would assume an attitude so strained, but it is so.

Hypnotism shows of ancient vintage used to present hallucinated situations that were distressing, such as suggesting to a person that a swarm of bees are buzzing about him; he will not only see and hear them, but he will go through violent antics to beat them off. Or a subject would be told that there are rats in the room, and the suggestion would wake up a train of imagery in the subject's mind which is immediately projected outward in an expressive display of appropriate gestures of aversion and corresponding movements of avoidance. Another test of terror that was performed by the old-age hypnotists was that the subject was being electrocuted. And imagine the fear depicted on the face of a subject when he believes he is about to be attacked by a tiger!

Needless to say, such suggestions inspiring terror are strictly taboò in the modern hypnotism show. Make it a consciencious rule that suggestions that present terror, horror, pain, and mental and physical disturbances of any kind must never be made. As a contemporary hypnotist, your entire entertainment is aimed at pleasantness and fun, with an emphasis on calming suggestions that are good for the subject. This 20th century approach is what places the modern hypnotism show in an entirely new light as purposeful entertainment, and makes it a worthwhile art form in every way.

Hallucinations of all the senses and delusions of every conceivable kind can be easily suggested to a good subject. Just how real these effects are to the subject is evidenced in experiments where the image of the hallucination has been caused to double by a prism or mirror, magnified by a lens, and in many other ways behaves optically like a real object.

In suggesting an hallucination say that of a flying bird, the suggested approach of the object causes contraction of the pupils, and vice versa. At the same time, there is often convergence of the axis of the eyes, as it a real object were present.

Subjects will eat a potato for a peach, or drink something bitter for soda water. He may be thrown into a state of intoxication by being caused to drink a glass of water under the impression that it is gin; or he may be restored to sobriety by the administration of gin under the guise of an antidote for drunkenness. In these cases, the expression of the face induced by the suggested perception corresponds so perfectly that a better effect would scarcely be produced if the real article were used.

Various physiological effects can be produced in the state of hypnosis. A subject can be caused to weep and shed tears on one side of the face and laugh with the other. The pulse can be quickened or retarded, respiration slowed or accelerated, and perspiration can be produced - - all by suggestion. Even the temperature can be affected. Thus it has been observed that if a subject is told he is very warm his pulse rate will increase and his face becomes flushed. Or, if a person is told that he is standing on ice he feels cold at once. "Gooseskin" can be produced by the suggestion of a cold bath. Hunger and thirst can be created, and other functions increased or retarded.

The mind can be so concentrated upon a physiological process as to stimulate that process to normal activity, so as to produce pathological effects or disease. For instance, a blister can be caused on a sound and healthy skin by applying a postage stamp and suggesting that it is a strong mustard plaster. Posthypnotic experiments have been performed in which a key or coin has been placed upon the skin of a subject with the suggestion that five minutes after awakening a blister will appear at the spot where the key or coin had been placed, and be of corresponding size and shape. The key or coin is then removed, and the subject awakened, having no conscious knowledge of the suggestion given, but at the appointed time the blister appears shaped as the object.

On the other hand, blisters and burns have been modified by suggestion. Mere local redness of the skin is easily produced by suggestion, and can be seen to appear in a few minutes by watching the subject.

Naturally, several organs can be influenced by suggestion at the same time. Tell the hypnotic, "Here is a rose." At once your subject not only sees, but feels and also smells the rose. The suggestion here affects sight, feeling and smell at the same time.

When the delusion is positive, the hypnotic believes he sees what does not exisit; when it is negative he fails to recognize the presence of an object really placed before him. An excellent experiment is to suggest to the subject that on awaking he will not be able to see you, although he will see everybody else. The subject on being awakened from hypnosis can hear and feel you, but he fails entirely to see you. The effect is quite weird, and your seem literally to have become "The Invisible Man." When speaking to him you will observe his head and eyes turn in direction of your voice, but you are completely invisible to him. His eyes appear to look right through you. This is a negative hallucination of sight. Similarly, it may be suggested that the subject is deaf to certain words, but not to others.

The production of reddening and bleeding of the skin in hypnotized subjects suggested by tracing lines or pressing objects thereupon, puts in a new light the accounts handed down to us of the stigmata of the cross appearing on the hands, feet, sides, and foreheads of certain mystics.

Also, it is possible to nullify pain through hypnotic suggestion. Before the advent of chemical anesthetics, hypnosis was used in major operations, and today is considerably employed in dental practice.

It is doubtful that you as a hypnotic entertainer will have much occasion to make use of these physiological effects of which hypnosis is capable, but they do serve to show its power. Such phenomena belong more. to the field of the physician and present superlative insight into an understanding of psychosomatic diseases.

Posthypnotic Suggestion

This phenomena of hypnosis is so important it deserves a section of it own. In this regard, consider the sense of time.

A time sense seems to be an innate mental power that people have. Some persons seem pretty well able to guess the time correctly no matter how suddenly the question is put to them. Posthypnotic suggestions make use of this time sense in being deffered suggestions given to the subject during hypnosis; such suggestions may be given to occur at a specified time.

It appears wonderful to most people that an event should take place at whatever time may have been suggested to the subject while in hypnosis, whether in one, two, or twenty-four hours, or 1,000 or 2,000 minutes, or in a month or more remote periods from the day on which a subject has been hypnotized. Bramwell has performed many successful experiments this way, as, for example, the following:

A woman was told that in so many thousands minutes, she was to write her name. She was not very well educated and, therefore, was not likely to work out the number of hours and minutes successfully; yet, at the time appointed, she wrote her name, and was surprised to find what she had done. In another case, he told a young lady to draw a picture after the lapse of 4,355 minutes, In spite of the fact that she had forgotten all about the suggestion, she fulfilled it accurately.

When the mind is made up to perform a certain action at a certain time, the idea is then dismissed from the mind; but if the subconscious has been properly trained, at the definite time, or reasonably near it, the action will be performed, although neither the thought of the time nor the idea of performing the action may have been in the mind from the moment that the resolution was taken and was put on one side to make room for other ideas. Here in these time experiments with posthypnotic suggestion, the creative hypnotist has some phenomena that really savors of the miraculous.

Sometimes no definite time is given, but it is suggested that at a time marked by a signal, a certain event is to take place. The moment the signal occurs (psychologists refer to such signal as "cue"), the subject who until then seems in a perfectly normal waking condition, will experience the effect of the suggested event. The conducting of such experiments are simple, as for example:

Suggest to the hypnotic, "When you awaken from hypnosis you will feel perfectly normal in every way, but when I touch the lobe of my ear you will experience an irresistable impulse to leave your chair, walk to the center of the room, and stretch yourself. You will have no memory of this command when you awaken, but the moment I touch the lobe of my ear you will immediately do as you have been directed."

Awaken the subject, and shortly touch the lobe of your ear and watch what happens.

The subject will respond as you instructed him in the trance, yet in his present state he will have no recollection at all of these posthypnotic directions. When questioned as to why he performed such an act, he will usually pass it off with a shrug, or else will rationalize about it, commenting that he just felt like stretching. In actual fact, the posthypnotic impulse is so powerful that the subject was unable to resist the performance of the suggested action the moment your "cue" set off the response.

In the same manner, you can rehypnotize your subject by the posthypnotic command that when you give a certain signal that he will instantly return again to the hypnotic sleep. This method of rehypnotizing the subject by posthypnosis functions as an important test for entertainment use as a demonstration of "instantaneous hypnotism," as you will learn. In such an effect, you have merely to give your subject a posthypnotic suggestion that when you point your finger at him, he will go instantly deep alseep. Suddenly, at a later time, point your finger at him and witness the striking reaction. Tests making use of posthypnotic suggestion are of great interest to audiences.

Another posthypnotic test of this same order is to hypnotize a number of subjects, and give them all the posthypnotic suggestion that when you drop a handkerchief they will immediately go sound asleep and instantly collapse. Awaken your subjects, stand them in a row. Then drop the handkerchief. They fall like rag-dolls to relaxed bundles of sleeping humanity. It's an effective experiment.

As a performing artist of hypnotism, you must naturally avoid all posthypnotic suggestions that excite or point ridicule towards the subject. Whatever you do, *do it with dignity.*

Through posthypnotic suggestion you can limit the subject's entering of hypnosis only to specific times that are mutually desired. You can likewise use it to cause resistance to hypnotic influence or increase it. States of mind can be affected, the subject made happy, sad, etc. Hunger and thrist or loss of appetite can be induced, personal character may be influenced. In general, with a good subject, all of the effects which can be produced in hypnosis can be equally produced in the posthypnotic state.

The Extraordinary Phenomena of Hypnotism.

The hypnotic phenomena you will learn in this section is of especial value to the entertainer as there are decided elements of mystery surrounding such. Let us first consider the conditions of hyperaesthesia of the senses and the accentuation of the innate mental qualities that may be produced in hypnosis.

Taking a normal subject in the hypnotic state and blindfolding him, one of the first observations that can be made refers to the probable existence of a "human aura," for by holding one or more fingers near any part of the subject's body or head, without coming in actual contact, that part will be moved in the direction in which the finger is slowly drawn. An ordinary horseshoe magnet, held similarly, produces a like result. Subjects have been found so sensitive to this influence of the magnet, that even though they were unaware that such an instrument was in the room, complained of unpleasant sensations, when the magnet was held near the back of their head.

Bramwell says on this point, "The enigmatic reports of the effect of magnets, even if they due, as many contend, to unintentional suggestion on the operator's part, certainly involve hyperaestehetic perception; for the operator seeks as well as possible to conceal the moment when the magnet is brought into play, and yet the subject not only finds it out that moment in a way difficult to understand, but may develop effects which (in the first instance certainly) the operator did not expect to find."

Magnets seem to give off effects very similar to that produced when passes are made with the hands. Here may be one of the reasons why passes are so valuable to use in your hypnotizing technique, as many subjects seem able to feel plainly a tingling sensation as the hands pass over their body.

Hollander writes on this point, "There is no doubt in my mind but that a magnet gives off some force which can be felt by a hypnotized subject, and that our body, particularly at the fingers's ends, exerts a similar influence. I became convinced of this by placing a hypnotized subject in a completely darkened room, then letting him open his eyes and describe what he saw. I held a magnet suspended in my hand at the poles of which he perceived a luminous appearance, and, when holding out my fingers, he described similar luminous emanations proceeding from my fingertips.

"The magnetic, or odylic influence is characterized, like heat, light, and electricity, as being sent forth in all directions, and by its emanations being luminous to sensitive persons, and most persons when in hypnosis can see it in daylight. I would here, in recommending the repetition and prosecution of these attractive researches by enquirers, urge on them the absolute necessity of following the conditions laid down.

"In order to see the odylic light, for example, not only must the subject be sensitive, but the darkness must be absolute, and if not at once successful, the sensitive should remain in darkness for an hour. Not the smallest gleam of light must be allowed to enter the darkend room. None of the audience should go out or come in during the experiment; for if the door be opened, the admission even for an instant of light from the next room may spoil the performance.

It is not unlikely that the human organism is a radioactive body, for if our experiments do not deceive us, the body emits rays which can be seen and felt by sensitive persons. There appears to be a "human aura" which extends from the body for a distance, some say a yard, and gradually fades away, And the aura of each person is seen to be colored according to the vibrations belonging to his prevailing mental states. That these rays can be seen I have already shown. The following is an experiment which I have often repeated, which would prove that they can also be felt:

"A hypnotized and blindfolded subject is made to distinguish a person's hand from a dozen others, when held above his or hers at a distance of six inches or less for a few seconds. This can be done with great success, and if you give numbers to the different persons present, the subject will, after a time, even recognize when the hand of No. 5 or 7 or any other, comes around again."

In experimenting with any of these mysterious "forces" which are admitted by those who believe in them to be very tenuous, your handling of suggestion must be applied carefully as such falsify results.

Other extraordinary hypnotic effects can be found in increasing the hypnotic's ability to see and hear to a hyperdegree.

Here is a fascinating experiment in these supersensitized hypnotic abilities. Take a deck of cards and have a card selected. Its name is noted. Then hand it to your subject back upward and tell him that it is a picture of his mother or wife, that he will be able to recognize and locate that picture under any conditions, and at any time. Then mix the card in the deck and hand the entire pack, backs uppermost, to the subject. One by one he will run through the cards, looking at the backs of each in turn, until finally stopping at one card which he will declare is the photo. On turning the card over, it will be found the correct one.

The explanation of this surprising demonstration is that every playing card, no matter how new or seemingly unmarked, has on it some minute difference which sets it apart from its neighbors. In this experiment, in the course of the illusion of seeing the suggested picture, the subject interprets into the illusion these minute differences, and through hypersensitized abilities he is able to distinguish that card by its back alone from amongst all of the others; the hypersensitized observing of the particular nearly invisible variations of that card calling into being the suggested illusion. Thus the card is located.

Extra Sensory Perception in Hypnosis

TELEPATHY. There are many interesting experiments in ESP that you can try with the entranced subject. Begin by suggesting to the hypnotic that he will feel an electric-like tingling sensation from your fingers as you pass them down his arm without contact, and, as he feels it, that his arm will slowly rise up from his lap.

Make passes down his right arm from the elbow to the fingers, and slowly his arm will rise. Then repeat the experiment, this time making passes down his left arm until that hand, too, lifts up.

Now explain that you are not going to tell him over which hand you are making the passes, but that as he feels the tingling sensation he is to raise that hand accordingly. Experiment with this test a few times to see if the subject can correctly determine over which hand you are making the passes. Then suggest that he will feel the same sensations in his hands merely when you think of his raising up either of his hands, and that he is to lift the hand in which he feels the tingles.

Now concentrate on his lifting either his right or left hand, as desired. In transmitting a telepathic impulse, such as lifting of a hand, do not particularly say over and over to yourself, "Lift your hand, lift your hand," *rather visualize in your mind an image of the subject actually lifting up the specific hand.*

Next have the hypnotic stand up with his feet together, explaining that he will feel an impulse to take a step forewards or a step backwards, as the case may be, and that when he senses such he is to step in that direction. Then flip a coin, if it comes up "heads" concentrate on him stepping forward; if "tails" then backwards. Keep track of your results and see how he does in relation to successful telepathic experience.

Take two subjects, hypnotize them and suggest they are in rapport; that one is the transmitter and the other the receiver. Touch the hand of the "transmitter" and tell him to concentrate on the other subject lifting the corresponding hand. Then the "receiver" is told that he is to lift up his hand that he feels a mental impulse to raise. Perform the test a number of times and tabulate your results.

Generally speaking, telepathic ideas of movements are the

simplest to transmit, but you can also experiment with cards, numbers, colors, pictures, letters of the alpabet, and words. *Whatever experimenting you elect to do, always make sure that your hypnotized subject understands exactly what test is being performed and what is expected of him.*

I have found the following hyperaesthetic method of hypnotizing useful for ESP experimenting:

Arrange a blue light and direct it so it shines over the forehead of your subject as he lies prone on a couch. Take your seat beside him and have him gaze into your eyes. See Fig. 33

Then begin making passes towards his face gently, and very softly suggest that his eyes are becomming heavy and are closing. When his eyes are closed, make passes over his face, while suggesting that he will go to sleep and on down into a deep trance.

In applying this method of hypnotizing, keep your verbal suggestions to an absolute minimum. Your whole approach must be extremely genteel, actually ascetic. You are attempting to arouse extra sensory perceptive abilities, so concentrate on mental commands by visualizing your subject going to sleep and passing on down, step by step, deeper and deeper into trance.

Next, stand beside your subject and while leaning over him make long passes starting at his head and going over the entire length of his body, ending at the feet. In making these passes, keep your hands about six inches away from his body and extend your fingers tensely outstretched while visualizing a "magnetic" current" passing out of them. Soon you will actually seem to experience a magnetic tingling-like sensation in your fingertips. See Fig. 34.

Then direct your extended fingers towards your subject's forehead, and, while making short circular stroking passes, visualize the transmission of the odylic influence, as shown in Fig. 35.

Fig. 33   Fig. 34

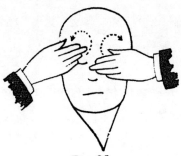

Fig. 35

As you make these passes, concentrate continuously on your mental suggestions of the subject going to sleep down deep into hypnosis. Keep your attention rapt and intent, and your eyes fixed on your subject. Then bring your hands on slowly down his body in straight passes, stopping at the heart, at this point making further short circle-like passes. Make these circular passes without contact, about six inches above the body, and then continue on with the long passes down to his feet.

When you reach the feet, having completed the long passes down the entire length of the subject's body, violently give your hands a flipping motion as though you were throwing off from the fingers a sticky substance, turn your hands plams outward, and again approach your subject's head, turn your hands palm inward over his forehead and repeat the process of long passes over the full length of his outstretched body.

Continue these "magnetic passes" for about ten minutes, and when you feel your subject has reached a sufficient depth, proceed testing for ESP talents.

CLAIRVOYANCE. This is another Psi Power of the mind with which you can experiment. Clairvoyance meaning psychic visioning is of much interest. For such an experiment, place your subject into a hypnotic trance using the method just described.

When you feel the subject is deeply entranced take out your watch and swirl the hands so you will have no knowledge of the time at which they are set. Then without looking at it hold the watch face inward to his forehead, and tell him you want him to tell you what time it is; that he can see the face of the watch within his mind clearly. Request the subject to speak to you and tell you the time at which the watch is set at; that he can see the image clearly. If he says he cannot see it, ask him what you can do to make him see plainer. If he tells you anything, do exactly as he tells you.

If the subject does not tell you what to do, make some passes over his forehead, and ask him if he can now see plainer. If he says, "Yes," make a few more passes, and insist that he tell the time at which the watch is set. At this point you should be very emphatic. Force him to see!

Now try another experiment in clairvoyance. Write various numbers on different cards. Turn them face down and mix the cards so you have no idea of the numbers. Without looking at it, pick up a card and hold it to the subject's forehead, and see if he can tell you what the figure is. Also ask him to describe some place where he has been. If he gives you a good, clear description, then ask him about some place unknown to him, and check his description.

Performing experiments in ESP under hypnosis are fascinating. Do not expect to succeed every time you try, for if you did these would not be known as "wild talents of the mind" that are unpredictable. And remember, you must develop your subjects for such tests; try the process every day for a week or two on a subject before you pass judgement. Some subjects can never be developed. In fact, it seems that comparatively few persons are capable of entering this clairvoyant state for it is an exceptional mental talent. You may have to try ten or fifteen subjects before you find one that is suitable, and when you do find a hypnotic who promises something in this direction do not use him in other tests, cultivate all of his hypnotic efforts in the psychic direction, and the more you practice on such feats the better he will become to the amazement of everyone.

These tests in the extraordinary phenomena of hypnotism are rather too experimental to be used during the general hypnotism stage show, but they are splendid for entertaining intimate groups who enjoy participating in ESP and exploring the wonders of the mind.

10
How to Awaken the
Hypnotized Subject

The phase of hypnotism that the general public seems most to worry about is the awakening of the subject from hypnosis. The question is frequently asked, "Will the person awaken safely after being hypnotized."

There are circulated far too many wild stories of how persons have been hypnotized and failed to reawaken. A physician having to be called in to awaken them. Actually, in hypnosis a subject is not unconscious in the first place, so there is really nothing to awaken them from other than to shift the hypnotic level of consciousness back to normal consciousness again. This is easily accomplished simply by using suggestions.

Since hypnosis is induced by a process of suggestion affirming the condition of hypnosis, it stands to reason that the reversing of the process will remove the hypnosis. As suggestions of "sleep" are often employed in bringing about hypnosis, just the reverse suggestions of "awakening" are used to terminate the condition. In this regard, as the subject is highly suggestible in the hypnotic state and is reacting in a manner that a sleeping person is expected to act, plan your awakening of the subject in exactly the same gentle manner you would use in awakening a person from normal sleep.

A foremost reason for there ever being any difficulty in awakening the hypnotic lies within faulty handling by an unskilled operator. For instance, I have watched a hypnotist make use of a slow, methodical method of inducing hypnosis applying it with great care, and then in awakening the subject become bombastic, clapped his hands by the subject's ear like thunder, and shouted a loud, "Wake up!" Under such a stimulus, some subjects literally leap out of their seats. Who wouldn't?

Such inconsiderate handling is ridiculous. With such an indelicate method of awakening the subject being employed it is little to be wondered at that a fear of the removal of hypnosis has developed.

After all, the hypnotizing process a shift in consciousness which is analogous to sleep, and how would you feel if someone so violently awakened you from sound slumber? Accordingly, *make it your rule in removing hypnosis to make the shift back to normal consciousness always in a gradual manner, never a sudden shock.*

If you will just keep in mind that in inducing hypnosis you presented your suggestions slowly and with care, and apply this same gentle and serene approach to the removal of the trace, you will minimize any possible difficulty. *And, remember, as a hypnotist it is your obligation to always awaken your subject feeling better than he did when you commenced hypnotizing him.* To that end, follow these directions in detail for the pleasant removal of hypnosis and the awakening of the subject:

Having caused all the suggestions of your final hypnotic experiment for the session to fade away from the mind of your subject, and suggested that he is resting calmly and peacefully, present these suggestions, "In a moment I am going to awaken you, and when you wake up you will feel just fine, relaxed and refreshed, and good all over. Now, I am going to count very slowly from one to five, and with every count you will awaken gradually – more and more -- until by the time I reach 'five' you will be wide awake. And when you wake up, you are going to feel just wonderful. You've had the best sleep and rest you have ever experienced, and your going to awaken in a few seconds now just feeling fine, full of vim, vitality, and pep – just feeling swell! All right now, I'm starting to count, so get ready to wake up. *One, two* . . . you are beginning to awaken now; beginning to wake up. *Three.* . .your eyes are opening; you want to move about and stretch. *Four.* . .waking up. *And Five!* Wake up. . .you are wide awake and just feel fine!"

Under the influence of these pleasant suggestions, your subject will gradually awaken, open his eyes, move about, stretch himself, and will be fully awakened *just felling fine!*

Note how gradual this handling of the awakening in removing hypnosis has been. How gentle and considerate it is of the subject's well-being. The subject is *set* for the awakening before it even begins, he expects it and is awaiting it.

Note, also, how suggestions during this awakening process constantly stress that he will awaken feeling fine and good all over.

In concluding this chapter on How To Awaken the Hypnotized Subject, I will point out a basic fact regarding hypnosis: *there is never any danger of the subject not awakening from the hypnotic trance, as left entirely to himself, even without awakening suggestions, the subject will simply pass from hypnosis into natural sleep, and will awaken of his own accord in due time.*

11
Some Theory
on Hypnotism

It has often been said about electricity, anyone can use it but no one knows exactly what it is. The same can be said about hypnotism, and, as a student, it is but natural that you should ask the question, "What is hypnotism?" For your understanding, I will give you some bits of personal theory on the subject.

Collin Bennet writes, "The practice of hypnotism is as straight-forward as its theory is involved. A good hypnotic subject can enter hypnosis almost as quickly as you can snap a switch and turn on an electric light. In each instance there is the effect, but just what has brought it about? What is electricity? What is hypnotism?

For an answer to that question, let us consider the power any idea *in which we believe* holds upon our lives. After all, we are the sum total of the thoughts we think, for our thoughts lead directly to our actions, and those thoughts which make up the very special personality which is represented in yourself by the are the deep rooted ideas which have been constantly hammered by environment, education, and experience into our mind. I use the word, "hammered" as it is expressive, for ideas mentally hammered-in either by force, repetition, or emotions are the special ideas that stick with us, and become a part of our personalities in forming the basis for our habits, fears, complexes, etc.

Such ideas so set in our nervous system produce unconscious responses. In other words, we have learned these special ideas that we no longer have to deliberately think about them, rather their action has become automatic. Such ideas, to use a psychological term, have become *conditioned* into the nervous system patterns of our lives – becoming habits, as it were. Or, in a sense, we might say that such ideas have been hypnotized into our mind, viz.:

Hypnosis may accordingly be regarded as that uncritical state of mind in which ideas will be largely accepted without qualification, and in which our nervous system may be conditioned most rapidly.

For example, suppose you hypnotize a subject and tell him what when he awakens from trance he will stutter. What happens on his removal from hypnosis? He stutters!

Now, while he is wondering about this unexpected disturbance in his speech, you assure him that is only your suggestions (or ideas) presented to him while he was hypnotized that are making him stutter, and ask that he try hard to overcome the influence. Occasionally, with such an understanding of the cause of the condition, the man can throw off the effect and speaks clearly again. But, if he has been deeply affected, he cannot do so even when he understands the cause of his problem. For the idea of his difficulty of speech has been so set in his nervous system that it is no longer under his voluntary control – it has become unconscious response, a habit. Through hypnosis he has been conditioned to stuttering, and a temporary oral neurosis (speech block) has been developed.

Now, let us consider stuttering in the case of a man in his normal state of mind. We reason with him·that there is nothing physically wrong with his speech, that his stuttering is entirely a mental condition, and assure him that he can master it.

He tries, but he still stutters.

We ask him to try harder. He does and, indeed, it seems that the harder he tries not to sutter the worse he stutters. Why? Because the idea of stuttering is so set as a habit in his mind that he no longer has voluntary control over it, and habits have a way of defying the will.

Is there any especial difference between our hypnotically induced stutter and this natural one? Basically there is none. The one was "sold" the idea of stuttering rapidly while in hypnosis, while the other was "sold" the idea of such behavior as a result of a long series of experiences in the course of his life. Since hypnotism can thus "sell" to the nervous system so efficiently ideas directly comparable to those developed in the process of years of daily living, it is self-evident the tremendous value and/or power that is invested in the condition.

Through this observation, it will be noted that hypnotism is obviously not some isolated mystical phenomenon, but is rather an induced state of mind with direct parallels to the normal development of our behavior patterns.

But what is hypnosis itself? Is it sleep? We have considered this question before but we will go over it again in connection with hypnotic theory. Hypnosis is not sleep and only resembles it from outward appearances due to the subject's imitation of the condition of sleep produced by the response to the suggestions of "sleep" which are employed in the induction technique.

Psychologically there is one great major difference between sleep and hypnosis. In sleep, the attention of the sleeper is diffused, and the rapport (avenue of communication to the mind) is enrapport–directed within himself. While in hypnosis, the attention of the subject is greatly amplified, and there is a direct and very strong rapport between the hypnotist and the hypnotized.

Hypnosis might thus be definited as a deliberately induced state of mind (an altered consciousness state of mind) in which the subject becomes extremely acute (beyond the acuteness of normal wakefulness). In this state, his attention span is extremely limited and the focus of awareness is entirely centered on the directed ideas (suggestions) of the hypnotist, which ideas are accepted uncritically and are responded to. And so sharply focused is this induced limitation of attention, coupled with the resultant shift in consciousness level, that when the trance is terminated a condition of amnesia can result from the experience.

Following this handling of theory in which hypnosis is regarded as an induced state of mind producing a condition of hyperattention, its ability to impress ideas (to condition) rapidly and powerfully upon the nervous system becomes evident. It is well known that in the process of learning the greater degree of attention which is focused upon the subject matter being learned, the greater the impression same makes upon the mind and the more throughly one learns it. In the hypnotic trance, therefore, having the very height of attention, we reach the pinnacle of the mind's ability to rapidly learn.

12
Questions and Answers
About Hypnotism

These are questions that are frequently asked about hypnotism. As an operator, it is well to have the answers on the tip of your tongue. There is worthwhile knowledge here.

WHAT PERCENTAGE OF PEOPLE CAN BE HYPNOTIZED. Every human being who is mentally sound can be influenced to some degree, some quickly and others with repeated trails. The degree of hypnotic influence varies with different persons. Some subject are capable of obtaining deep somnambulistic phenomena, even including posthypnotic, while others will respond only in lighter degree tests such as muscular catalepsy.

Taking an average of all humanity, one person in five (20% of the population) may be classified as being *a natural somnambulist* who has the innate ability to be deeply entranced on the first session. However, this percentage can be decidedly increased by working with a subject in a series of repeated inductions.

Being able to obtain deep hypnosis is a mental skill, and like developing proficiency in any skill, some persons have a natural talent while others have to learn the practicing way of repeated effort. As always. in the cultivation of any ability, "practice makes perfect."

WILL BEING HYPNOTIZED WEAKEN ONE'S WILL? This question is a "hangover" from the superstitious days of the old Svengali type of hypnotist who through histrionics appeared to master and dominate his subject, making the subject appear like a weak-willed puppet. Actually, even in such extreme cases, the domination of the will is more illusion than fact, for will has very little to do with hypnosis. It can be truthfully affirmed that imagination has far more to do with hypnosis than does will-power.

It can be definitely stated that hypnotism does not weaken the will. Indeed, it is possible through suggestion to stregthen and cultivate those traits of character usually associated with will-power, namely, increased determination of purpose, drive, better concentration, more forceful individuality, and self-confidence.

Directly associated with this question is the following:

IS A WEAK WILLED PERSON EASIER TO HYPNOTIZE THAN A STRONG—MINDED INDIVIDUAL? Decidedly not. The very factors that go into the making of a determined, forceful personality are the ones most necessary for the successful induction of hypnosis. Generally speaking, weak-willed persons are those considered incapable of seriously being able to concentrate for the successful pursuance of any idea, and, as such, are the worse possible hypnotic subjects.

The above comment is not meant to infer that superior intelligence is an indispensable factor (helpful as it frequently is) in achieving hypnosis. Rather than intelligence, reference is here made to the personality factor of an individual's emotional drive to pursue to its successful completion a given objective.

CAN A PERSON BE HYPNOTIZED AGAINST HIS WILL? Generally speaking a person must be willing in order to be hypnotized, as for hypnosis to be induced the ideas presented must be accepted into the mind as the center of attention. To be so centered in attention, it is obvious that the ideas must possess all absorbing interest. However it is possible for "an all absorbing interest" to be produced by trepidation as well as purpose, thus occasionally the entering of hypnosis does have the appearance of having been produced without the subject's consent. Psychologically, however, the subject is actually hypnotized by his own motivation.

Further, some special situations may arise where a person may seem to be influenced so automatically that it seems that he did not give his willing consent to be hypnotized. Such incidents are rare, but they do occur. In such a case, the answer lies in the fact that consent to entering hypnosis may be an unconscious motivation as well as a deliberated one.

IS IT POSSIBLE FOR A HYPNOTIST TO MAKE A SUBJECT PERFORM AN IMMORAL ACT? On this question, most contemporary authorities agree that a person's moral code under hypnosis remains unchanged from his moral code in his normal state. Remember, just because a person is hypnotized does not imply that he has become another individual in any sense. He is still entirely his own man. What moral scruples the subject shows in his normal state of mind he will also exhibit under hypnosis. Indeed, a hypnotized subject if often even more scrupulous than one awake, for the subconsciousness of an individual seems to sense any possibilities of danger and rallies quickly to the protection of the individual -- either by immediately awakening the subject from the trance or by a flat refusal to respond to the immoral suggestion.

ARE WOMEN MORE EASILY HYPNOTIZED THAN MEN? Not especially. The sexes seem about equal in their overal responsiveness to hypnosis. While the more emotional natures of woman can tend to make them more susceptible to entering quickly deep hypnosis, this very quality can also produce a self-consciousness which is distrubing to concentration on the suggestions.

Men, on the other hand, tend to accept the experience in a more experimental and matter-of-fact way, and more readily comply with directions.

13
Selected Tips for Successful Hypnotizing

This chapter will round out your knowledge of hypnotism, provide you with additional instructions, and, also, function as a transition into the next section of this book which features stage hypnotism in which you will learn how to hypnotize groups of people and present an outstanding entertainment. All of this material is important to your developing professional status as a hypnotist.

Use Preliminary Experiments

Generally speaking, in working with a group, before you try for trance phenomena, it is well to commence with some of the waking suggestion experiments you have learned such as drawing the subject backwards, locking hands together, etc. In doing so, explain that before you hypnotize anyone you wish to ascertain which of the subjects can concentrate best, and work with as many subjects as possible in these preliminary tests before you attempt to induce hypnosis. This is expert handling and provides you with an opportunity to locate whom among the group are the most susceptible subjects. Use these subjects for your first experiments in hypnosis as leaders of the group. There is good psychology here as your success in hypnotizing your first subjects will bring you success with the others as well.

Establish Confidence

Whenever it is possible, let a new subject see you hypnotize someone whom you have hypnotized previously before you try to influence him This immediately develops the potential subject's confidence in your ability to hypnotize, and gives him an appreciation of the art.

Do Not Boast

Nobody likes an egoist. Always approach your work as a hypnotist in a modest, confident manner. To boast of your ability is to develop a challenging attitude in your subjects, and can undermine the success of your performance. Adopt the manner of the successful physician.

Keep Your Promises

Never under any circumstances be so untrustworthy as to have your subjects do anything you have told them you would not do. Many subjects will request that if they are hypnotized you will promise not to make them do embarrassing acts. When you give your promise to follow their wishes, always honor that trust.

Revolving the Head in Inducing Hypnosis

This interesting process will sometimes hypnotize a person when other techniques fail. It is good one to know. Place the fingers of your left hand on the back of the subject's head, pressing inward and upward at the base of the brain. Place the thumb of your right hand at the root of his nose and your fingers on his left temple. Now revolve his head slowly in a circle, as you present your "sleep formula."

Tapping on Top of the Head to Induce Hypnosis

Another effective technique for inducing hypnosis is to gently tap on the top of the front part of the subject's head. Do this very lightly, but with a firm pressure, and at regular intervals like the ticking of a clock. Give suggestions of "sleep" during this tapping. If the subject becomes very sleepy, but does not quite enter hypnosis, then let your fingers rest firmly on the top of his head, and tell him that soon he will be breathing very deeply and will be fast asleep. Then commence yourself to breathe very deeply right beside his ear. The subject responding to this technique will frequently drop into trance at once.

Pressing Upon the Eyelids to Induce Hypnosis

When the eyes of the subject are closed, steady pressure applied at the corners of the eyes, near the root of the nose, will often assist in bringing about hypnosis.

Using a Combination of Methods to Induce Hypnosis

Hypnosis may be induced by suggestion, bright objects, or by passes. A combination of processes will usually hypnotize more persons than any single one device.

Supplementing Suggestions to Induce Hypnosis

When giving suggestions that the arms feel heavy, by way of an example for using this technique, it is often well to press upon the arms and when you tell your subject that everything is dark, put your hands over his eyes. Such devices to intensify the force of your suggestions are always valuable.

How to Transfer Hypnotic Control

You can transfer the hypnotic control of the subject from yourself to another person if you wish. To do this, after the subject is in hypnosis, suggest, "You will now follow the suggestions that Mr. So and So (person's name) gives you, and will respond to his suggestions just as you have to mine."

As you present these "transfer of control suggestions" to the subject have the persons to whom the transfer is being made place his hand on the forehead of the subject; this identifies the person and increases the strength of the transfer control.

How to Check for Hypnosis in a Subject

There are subtle observations which you can make that provide indications of the ensuing hypnotic trance state. To this end, watch your subject closely. Usually when hypnosis sets-in, there will be noted a sort of drooping about the corners of the mouth. This is often coupled with a little intake gasp of breath, and the subject's breathing will become deep and regular as in sleep. Then gently lift up one of his closed eyelids as you suggest that the action will send him down yet deeper to sleep. If he is deeply hypnotized, usually his eyeballs will be found rolled upward under the upper lid.

It is important that you learn how to recognize these physical symptons of hypnosis as they will guide you in the correct giving of suggestions. In time your interpretation will become instinctive.

Gradation of Response to Hallucinations

It is easier to decieve the sense of taste than it is the senses of sight and hearing. A suggestion that the subject will experience a bitter tase in his mouth is much more certain to work than one that he will see a landscape unfolding before him when he opens his eyes. This principle of progressively arranging the hallucinations from the simpler to the more complex is important in developing a new subject.

Illusions Versus Hallucinations

It is easier to make a subject believe that one object is another object (as an illusion) than it is to make him believe that an object exists in empty space (as an hallucination). For example, you can readily make him see a blue carpet as a pool of water more easily than you can an elephant in an empty room. Use this device of utilizing a stimulating object resembling the suggested illusion when first creating optical deceptions.

How to Produce Complete Body Catalepsy

Large groups of muscles can be made cataleptic as well as smaller muscle groups. For such a demonstration, after you have placed the subject in hypnosis, have him stand up straight and tell him that the muscles of his entire body are becoming stiff and rigid, so stiff and rigid that they will not bend. As you give these suggestions, make passes over his body, pressing in here and there on the muscles of his arms, legs, and chest as though to tighten them, and say, "You are absolutely rigid." Then suggest emphatically, "RIGID!" Your subject will become stiff like a pole and be unable to bend in any direction. You have produced a condition of complete body catalepsy.

When you are ready to remove the cataleptic state, tell him that his muscles are now beginning to lossen and relax, and are becomming flexible and normal in everyway. When his muscles are again relaxed, awaken him, and the experiment is complete.

Techniques for Deeper Hypnosis

As mentioned, stage hypnotists aim to produce deep hypnosis so subjects will perform effectively, however it must be born in mind that there is actually very little stability to the depth of hypnosis, and often a subject will drift from deep trance into lighter stages. For this reason, it is well for the operator to continually incorporate into his experiments repeated induction procedures such as suggesting that when such and such a test is performed it will send the subject on down yet deeper to sleep and/or hypnosis, or that as the subject's eyes open and he sees such and such hallucination that it will send him on down deeper and deeper into hypnosis.

This principle of letting the operation of each hypnotic test be related in effect to the deeping of the hypnosis is of great importance to the stage hypnotist in the continual maintenance of deep trance. You will recognize the principle as the *compounding of suggestions* which we have studied thoroughly. For purposes of deeping hypnosis, you can make use of the handling I advised of before in which it is suggested to the hypnotic that he will find his arms stuck in the air when he awakens (posthypnotic suggestion), but that when you snap your fingers his hands and arms will instantly relax and fall to his lap, and that when they touch his lap he will instantly go down even deeper asleep.

Another process for the development of deep hypnosis is to allow the subject(s) sufficient time to orient himself to both the induction of hypnosis as well as to the suggestions given in the hypnotic state. This is especially true when the suggestions are of a complex nature; the subject must not be pressed to produce the desired phenomenon too rapidly. Complex phenomena must be brought about gradually, step-by-step if necessary.

The hypnotist must recognize that trance induction and trance utilization are two entirely different things, and the subject must be allowed the opportunity to orientate himself in both phases. This principle is important in developing the subject's maximum response to the suggestions, but, also, because if sufficient time is not allowed the subject for orientation to the suggestion the hypnosis tends to shift to lighter stages. Psychologically this is an attempt on the part of the subject to secure the aid of his normal conscious mental processes to assist in the performance of the suggestions if the hypnotist has not sufficiently allowed time for this proper comprehension by the hypnotic. Conversely, complete orientation to each suggestion tends to deepen the trance.

Time for performance is not the only factor in orientating the subject sometimes the situation itself must be manipulated. In this regard, the stage hypnotist can assist the subject's orientation to certain suggestions by associatate suggestions of either familiar experience or situations, so that the suggestions being operated upon fall upon familiar ground. In practice, suggestions of when you do such and such it will seem exactly like what you have done repeatedly all of your life, or the suggestions you are having fun on the stage performing such and such, are example of this handling.

Further deepening of hypnosis occurs when the hypnotist allows his subject(s) the complete opportunity to respond to the suggestion fully to its greatest potential before proceeding on to another experiment. The hypnotic is "trained" this way, thus, to react to each suggestion with maximum effectiveness of response rather than to slur over from one response to another if the suggestions are too rapidly presented to allow adequate time for each to occur fully.

The stage hypnotist must recognize the fact that when two or more suggestions conflict, the one which was given first, in the greatest depth of hypnosis, is the one most likely to carry effect. In this regard, the operator must always keep in mind that first rule for the giving of successful suggestions is to always remove the operation of each suggestion fully before going on to a new suggestive effect. Failure to do this can give rise to psychological difficulties to the subject(s) as well as to the smooth running of the stage show. Especially in relation to subject well-being is this important.

The stage hypnotist should always integrate the subject's needs into the suggestions being given, as the more a suggestion satisfies such needs the better it will be acted upon. Thus associating suggestions of possible benefits being reaped as the result of the response to the suggestions is of great value in intensifying the phenomena. A practical application of this principle, that I often use is to associate in the subject's mind a useful skill that he will develop as a result of having achieved success in the hypnotic test suggested. For example, by saying, "If you are able to achieve this hypnotic test of reducing your body sensations in going down into deep hypnosis, you will have at the same time, developed the necessary ability to remove pain sensations from your teeth the next time you go to the dentist.

This principle of presenting a practical goal that the subject will be achieving as a result of his efforts to be an effective hypnotic can go a long ways in motivating towards depth in hypnosis. By continually placing into operation the various techniques that have been here outlined, the hypnotist will be assured of the developing and maintaining of the deepest possible levels of trance and the maximum responsiveness to the suggestions by the subject(s).

Fractional Hypnotism

As a related process of maintining and deepening hypnosis, the operator will find this technique most effective. It offers a method of deeping the hypnotic state in the subject(s) by a series of rapid consecutive hypnotizations. The method can be effectively used with group hypnotizing on the stage or with solo subjects; each short hypnotization tending to cause the subject(s)

93

to become more and more suggestible, and favors the induction of deeper hypnosis on each successive experience.

In practice, the subject(s) is first hypnotized in the usual manner. It is then suggested, "In a moment, I will tell you to awaken and when I do you will wake up but will immediately begin to feel very sleepy again. You will find it difficult to keep your eyes open and stay awake. And, as you look at me, your eyes will gradually close again, you will breathe deeply, and you will return to a deep sleep, deeper asleep than ever before. All ready now, at the count of 'three' you will wake up. One two,*three!* Wake up!"

Your subject(s) will thus be awakened from the first induction for a few moments, and, as he looks at you and you continue your suggestions, will again close his eyes and reenter hypnosis. Proceed to give some further deeping of trance suggestions, and then again repeat this awakening and immediate returning to hypnosis process.

This procedure performed three or four times on the subject(s) will be found to effect many people who at first were only lightly influenced, and to produce a deep trance. This process of hypnotizing, awakening, rehypnotizing, awakening, rehypnotizing, awakening, rehypnotizing in rapid succession makes use of repeated posthypnotic suggestions which are powerful in inducing deep hypnosis.

How to Give Posthypnotic Suggestions to the Hypnotic

We have discussed this important phase of hypnosis previously. Here is a resume of the handling, viz.:

After you have placed your subject deeply in hypnosis, tell him very positively that at some definite time he will do some particular thing. For example you may suggest, "At one o'clock in the afternoon you will feel a desire to change your shoes for another pair that you believe will be more comfortable. You will not remember that I gave you this suggestion, but at precisely that time develop this incentive and will change the pair of shoes you have been wearing for another pair. And if anyone asks you why you did this, you will simply say, "Because the new pair is more comfortable."

On the stroke of one, the subject will develop the impulse and will change his shoes, and if asked about the matter will rationalize his actions, as you have suggested. An experiment such as this shows the spontaneous nature of responses to posthypnotic suggestions.

In giving posthypnotic suggestions, be sure they are clear, positive, and emphatic. While not always necessary, it is good practice to repeat such suggestions a time or so to be sure they are well understood by the hypnotic. Then awaken the subject, and, at the appointed time, he will perform as you have hypnotically instructed.

Use caution as to the character of the posthypnotic suggestions which you give the subject, being sure that they are not too difficult or precarious for him to perform. The whole secret of this posthypnotic influence consists in telling the subject, while he is in hypnosis, the thing you wish him to do when he awakens. As mentioned, it is well to repeat your posthypnotic suggestions several times so they are strongly emphasized. If he should fail to carry out the suggestions, you may be sure that the failure is due either to lack of conviction in the way you presented the suggestion, or that the subject was not in a sufficient depth of trance to experience successfully posthypnotic effects.

Increasing Hypnotic Susceptibility Via Posthypnotic Suggestion

Before awakening your subject, give him suggestions to the effect that the next time you attempt to hypnotize him that he will go immediately into hypnosis; that as he gazes into your eyes, he will enter the hypnotic trance immediately. Such posthypnotic suggestions will increase your ease in hypnotizing the subject at a later period.

How to Hypnotize in Natural Sleep

It is possible to turn natural sleep into hypnosis by this process:

Go quietly to the sleeping person and speak gently, in a whisper, saying, "You are sleeping soundly. Sleep. You are sleeping soundly. You are sound asleep and nothing will disturb you. You will not wake up as I talk to you, for you are going down deeper and deeper alseep. Sleep. Sleep deeply."

Repeat these suggestions of sleep several times.

If you notice any signs of the sleeper awakening, immediately desist; otherwise keep the suggestions up for three or four minutes. Then put your hand on the sleeper's head, and say to him, "You hear no sound except my voice for you are fast asleep."

Now ask him some simple questions, such as, "How do you feel?" or tell him that he smells a rose and ask if he smells its beautiful fragrance? Insist on a reply to your question until he answers it. When he does so without awakening, you may be assured that he is in the hypnotic state. You have converted natural sleep into hypnosis.

You can now proceed to present whatever suggestions you feel are worthwhile to the subject. Usually suggestions benefitting the subject's well-being are given during the night. As you conclude the session, tell the subject to return to his normal, healthy sleep, that he will not have been disturbed in anyway, and will not remember the transfer from sleep to hypnosis.

When he awakens the next morning, he will have no memory whatever of the experience. This is a good technique to know, especially for parents who wish to use it to give helpful suggestions to their children.

How to Hypnotize Children

Children make excellent hypnotic subjects, but to effectively hypnotize them you must place your suggestions on the child's level. To instruct a child to relax his eye muscles, for instance, means little; you must speak in his language.

In working with children, hypnosis can be most readily produced by playing the "lets pretend to play act." Children are always pretending they are cowboys and Indians, or cops and robbers, etc. So if you ask a child to pretend, he instantly knows just what you mean for him to do. You can use this approach for producing hypnosis quickly in children.

Ask the child if he likes to play games. The answer in the affirmative say, "All right, I have a game to play with you, and if you learn to play it real good, it becomes a "Magic Game," and the nicest things can happen to you. Would you like to know how to play it?

Child responds.

"All right, its a game of pretend. You've played pretend haven't you? Pretending you're a cowboy, or maybe cops and robbers. You've played that game, haven't you? All right, I'll show you how to play this pretend game, and you do just like I tell you.

"Just open your eyes real wide, and I'll close them with my thumb and middle finger, as I draw my fingers down over your forehead and eyes. Now, just pretend that you can't open them. Pretend just as hard as you can. Are you pretending just as hard as you can? All right, I'll just snap my fingers and make it come true."

Snap your fingers.

"Now, even you tried to open your eyes, they wouldn't open, as long as you keep pretending. Try it and see, and the more you try, the less they will open. Now, just keep on pretending and some real nice things will happen to you."

The child is in hypnosis, as quickly as that. Now is the time to give him suggestions for improvement of his conduct, his manners, for getting better grades in school, or anything that will be of help to him. Or on the stage, he will preform all sorts of interesting tests if you explain such simply as a game he is taking part in.

To the child it seems that he is playing pretend, yet actually he is hypnotized and is responsive to your suggestions. Children respond very quickly to hypnosis, and do not generally need deepening techniques. As soon as they start pretending, there sense of judgement is by-passed, and they are ready for suggestions. You can try this experiment:

"Johnny (or whatever the child's name is), when I tell you to open your eyes you will open them wide, and an odd thing is going to happen. You will find that when you try to walk away you will not be able to lift your feet from the spot you are now in. You will try very hard to walk away, but the more you try, the more your feet will be stuck to the floor, until I snap my fingers and then they will come free right away. Now, that would be a funny thing to have happen, wouldn't it? So open your eyes now. How do you feel?"

Child answers, "Okay."

"That's fine. Now Johnnie, will you please bring me that dish from the table there."

The child tries to move, but cannot lift his feet to take a step. When ready to cancel the suggestion, just snap your fingers, and say, "Now, you can get the dish, and bring it to me."

Child brings you the dish, and again takes his seat. Again you drag your thumb and middle finger down over his eyes closing them, and tell the child to again pretend they are stuck and that he cannot open them.

Child will be unable to do so.

Now suggest, "Johnnie, when I have you open your eyes next time, and odd thing will happen in this game we are playing. Everytime you see me comb my hair, you will have a tickle in your back. And you will rub it, and the more you rub it, the more it will tickle; it will make you laugh because it is so funny. When I clap my hands, the tickle will stop. That's okay with you, isn't it?"

Child responds.

"All ready, let's play the game. Open your eyes!"

Comb your hair after you have the child's attention. He will begin to tickle, laugh, and rub his back. Comb your hair again, and the tickle will get more pronounced, until you cancel the suggestion by clapping your hands.

You can remove the child from the hypnosis by merely saying, "All right, the pretending game is over now. I will count to three, and at the count of 'three' you will open your eyes and be your bright, happy self, and just feeling fine."

Children will always respond to hypnosis if your suggestions are presented correctly. If you will make your suggestions something that will be fun for the child (or children you are performing with) there is no limit to the fascinating stunts you can present.

How to Prevent Other Persons from Influencing Your Subjects

If you do not wish anyone else to hypnotize your particular subject, while he is under hypnosis tell him that he cannot be hypnotized by anyone until the words, "Zambisi Zam" (or any word "cue" combination desired) are first given. This serves as a mental cue that the subject unconsciously awaits as the opening to his acceptance of the hypnotizing suggestions.

In this regard, never flatly tell a subject that he cannot be hypnotized again, as such might render him unresponsive to all future experiments. If he thinks he is too suseptible to the influence, you can tell him, while in hypnosis, that he cannot ever be hypnotized unless he, personally, expresses a wish to be.

On the Use of Passes to Awaken the Subject

Passes made in a downward direction are used to induce the trance, while passes made upward are used to remove it. Passes can thus be used to assist in the gentle awakening process in bringing the subject out of hypnosis. The procedure is to turn the palms upward, and starting about level with the subject's stomach move them upwards past his face. Repeat these upward passes several times in conjunction with the giving of your awakening suggestions. Blowing gently on the closed eyelids is also useful in awakening the subject.

On Awakening Difficult Subjects

Only rarely will you experience any difficulty in awakening a subject, but in such a case say to him, "All right now, I want you to wake up. I know you are sleepy and tired, but you MUST wake up now. You have slept long enough. Tell you what I will do. I will count very slowly from one to ten, and when I reach the count of 'ten' you wake up. Fair enough? Will you awaken at the count of ten?" If the subject does not answer, persevere until he does, and make him promise that he will wake up when you reach the count of "ten." Then continue, "All right then, here we go. One, two, three, four, five, six seven, eight, nine, TEN!" Just as you say "ten" clap your hands loudly together (in the case of a subject of this nature you need not worry about noise shocking his nervous system as he is the lethargic type,) and say, "WAKE UP! WAKE UP! ALL RIGHT, WIDE AWAKE NOW!" Keep striking your hands together, make upward passes, and give awakening suggestions until the subject is fully awake.

This process will awaken the most difficult subject.

Self-Induced Hysteria

There is a factor in relation to hypnotic awakening that you should understand. This is self-induced hysteria. We are all familiar with how teenagers at a Rock and Roll Concert will sometimes work themselves up into such a frenzy that they literally pass out. In such instance, the hypnotist has little rapport with his subject, as they have delibertly induced their own condition. Often the motivation for such is to secure attention by not awakening when told to. If a subject acts in this fashion, immediately remove attention from him Say, "Okay, go ahead and sleep as long as you want to. I'll place you aside so you can't bother the show any longer and no one can see you." Isolate the subject by themselves and leave them alone. You can be sure they will awaken in short order.

Awakening a Subject Someone Else Has Hypnotized

Occasionally you may be called upon to dehypnotize a subject that some inexperienced operator has hypnotized. The method is to proceed to gain rapport with the subject by the process of hypnotizing him personally even though he is already in hypnosis. To do this, place your hand on his head, repeat a "sleep formula" to him and then test him for response to your suggestions. After he has responded to a few tests, say very decidedly to him "Now when I tell you to do anything you will do it at once." Then give him a suggestion producing physical movement of some kind. After this response, apply the technique previously explained for awakening difficult subjects, and he will awaken readily to your command.

Always Awaken Subjects With Confidence

There are only two main reasons why a subject will not awaken readily from hypnosis (1) because of enjoying the hypnotic state so thoroughly that he hates to come out of it, and (2) because he has lost confidence in the operator. A hypnotized person is often very sleepy; to ask him to come immediately out of the trance sometimes seems just too much trouble, and hence the subject makes no immediate attempt to follow your command. But never for a moment lose confidence of your ability to awaken the subject. Remember, a hypnotized person is highly suggestible, and a betrayal of nervousness on your part over concern about awakening him can be interpreted as a suggestion that he is difficult to awaken, and such a suggestion is reacted to accordingly.

Always in performing all aspects of your hypnotic work be calm and collected, and keep in mind that a lack of confidence is as unfavorable to success in removing the trance as it is in producing it.

How to Hypnotize a Group of Subjects All At the Same Time

Have your subjects sit in a semicircle, while you take a position standing in front of them so everyone can see you easily. Tell all in the group to look directly at you. Pass your eyes around the semicircle so that each person feels that you are looking directly at him.

You now proceed to perform various hypnotic tests on the entire group exactly as you would with one subject. Having gained the attention of every person in the group, focus your gaze on no one person in particular, letting it rest about a foot above the head of your central subject, and give your suggestions forcefully towards this focused space.

Now tell them to put their hands together, to push on them

tightly, suggesting that when you count to "three" they will be unable to pull them apart. Count, "One, two, three," and state emphatically, "Now you cannot take your hands apart. Try, try hard, but they will not come apart.

Now tell them to put their hands together, to push on them tightly, suggesting that when you count to "three" they will be unable to pull them apart. Count, "One, two, three," and state emphatically, "Now you cannot take your hands apart. Try, try hard, but they will not come apart. All right now, when I snap my fingers they will instantly come apart." Snap your fingers and complete the test.

If you wish to put them into hypnosis, stand out in front and tell them to close their eyes and to think of sleep, going sound asleep, and suggest, "Close your eyes, close them tightly and think of sleep. Your head feels heavy and you are going sound asleep. Your limbs feel so heavy they are pressing down. You cannot move, you cannot feel anything. Your eyes are closed tightly, they will not open. You are sound asleep in hypnosis. You hear nothing but the sound of my voice, and it is sending you down, down, down deeper and deeper to sleep."

From this point, proceed with various experiments as you wish, concluding the session by suggesting, "All right now, you have all slept long enough. I will count slowly from one to five, and at the count of five you will all awake, be wide awake and feeling fine." Then count slowly from one to five and awaken the group.

This brief description of group hypnotizing will serve as a preamble to the technique. You will be studying this process in detail when the complete hypnotism show is dealt with in the following chapters.

Practice! Practice! Practice!

You now have the knowledge to make you an expert hypnotist, but the skill with which you apply that knowledge is entirely up to you. Hypnotism is exactly like any other performing art -- it is how you interpret and present it that counts. As those in the know say, "It is not what you do, it is how you do it."

So, practice diligently and develop your skill as a hypnotist. With practice comes perfection. Practice on single subjects. Practice on groups. Practice in private. Practice in public. Learn your hypnotic methods so thoroughly that they are second nature to yourself. Make your techniques as much a part of yourself as your most familiar actions are, so they occur almost automatically with complete smoothness and ease. It is by knowing hypnosis so well that you can then concentrate your attention on the showmanship and entertainment aspects of stage hypnotism.

Then, when you are thus confident of your ability, step out and you are ready for *Stage Hypnotism.*

PART TWO:
ENTERTAINING
WITH HYPNOTISM

THE MODERN HYPNOTISM SHOW IS A THOUGHT-PROVOKING FUN SHOW FOR ALL AGES. Here hypnotized high school students are reacting to exciting hypnotic experiences on the stage.

14
An Introduction
to Stage Hypnotism

The term stage hynotism is used synonymously to entertaining with hypnotism in performing situations such as parties, social gatherings, club groups, lectures, and stage shows. When you think about stepping out on a stage expecting to entertain an audience for a period of thrity minutes to a full evening with nothing for support but a group of empty chairs, it is assuredly an undertaking to make the stoutest showman pause and reflect. Indeed, it is the skill it takes to handle well such a presentation that has made stage demonstrations of hypnotism the very special events they are.

The qualifications for the successful stage hypnotist rate among the top in the entertainment profession, for stage hypnotism can unquestionably be cited as one of the most complex of all forms of entertainment to present, as two shows have to be given simultaneously (one for the subjects on stage and one for the spectators in the audience), while, at the same time, having to meet and master responsibilities imposed by audience participation situations.

Unlike other entertainers such as singers, dancers, magicians, etc., who once they have mastered their respective arts have their act entirely under their own control, the hypnotist's show is entirely one of audience participation and he relies completely upon the conduct of volunteers invited up from the audience itself. If the subjects respond and perform well he succeeds in producing superlative entertainment and his show is a success. BUT, conversely, if his subjects do not respond and perform well his show is a failure. It's a big BUT!

Many performers feel that relying upon the responses of volunteers to put a show over is too great a risk to take. *But it can be done one hundred percent sucessfully,* and I will instruct you from personal experience exactly how to do it. I will show you all the necessary insights and skills to make the stage presentation of hypnotism successful and reduce to the very minimum all possibilities of failure. For in truth, while in hypnotism you must always deal with the unpredictable aspects of the human mind the "cards can be stacked" in your favor to a sufficient extent that the success of your shows can be largely a certainty.

There are many advantages to the hypnotic act as entertainment. The fact that it takes skill to present raises its prestige value and entertainment appeal. Then, too, such a show is spectacular and production size in scope. And you need carry no props of equipment, *the audience, itself, providing all of the material for your performance.* All the performer need bring with him is his knowledge, which, when artfully applied, can produce a show without parallel in audience favor. For, hypnotism as entertainment has everything: comedy, mystery, drama; coupled with educational and thought provoking phenomena -- *and every show is different!* So complete is the appeal of the hypnotism show that, is properly handled, it is doubtful if any other entertainment is capable of creating more spontaneous interest and enthusiasm.

Are such goals worthy of achieving? If so, then study and practice well, for the presentation of stage hypnotism is a culmination of the skills of the lecturer, the psychologist, and the showman. Artistically blended they flow into the perfect presentation that lifts stage hypnotism from a novelty and places it among the arts.

The successful performance of hypnotism, upon the stage, calls for both a thorough knowledge of hypnotism and an understanding of showmanship. *Remember, your work as a stage performer is primarily to entertain,* and while you must be able to skillfully hypnotize you must be even more concerned with building and maintaining the interest of your audience.

In view of the dual nature of the work, entertaining with hypnotism obviously calls for a skilled craftsman. Let us consider, therefore, just what qualifications you will need to be a competent stage hypnotist, viz.

1. You must be thoroughly acquainted with hypnotic induction techniques and know how to produce all manner of hypnotic phenomena to the ends of skillfully implanting suggestions for the production of waking suggestion experiment and trance phenomena.

2. You must be a showman. By a showman is meant a qualified entertainer. As such, you must have good vocal delivery, poise, stage presence, audience understanding, a sense of timing, and dramatic ability. All of these qualities are essentials that form your background as a talented performer. *Remember, the ability to entertain is a skill that comes with practice, and the best teacher is experience.*

3. You must have a routine for your show. Nothing is more important to the stage hypnotist than to know *exactly* what he is going to do, what tests follow each other, and to proceed through the basic pattern of his show -- from start to finish with precision.

The hypnotism show is very similar to the stage play: it has an opening, a body, a climax, and a conclusion. The exact drama of your particular show depends largely upon yourself, though as hypnotic entertainment it is bound to flow along certain lines. *However, whatever your specific routine, it must be throughly learned and become as second-nature to yourself.*

Lest it seem that these qualifications for successful stage hypnotism loom somewhat overwhelmingly, let's pause a moment and consider a few of the factors that are working in your favor, factors that make entertaining with hypnotism not as difficult as it might at first appear.

In this regard, appreciate that the stage situation sets you in a glamourized position which automatically gives you prestige. Your advance advertising and publicity, your introduction, the audience expectation to witness hypnotic miracles, your acceptance as a professional hypnotist on stage as a performer -- you assuming the active role while spectators have the submissive -- are all factors from the very start which you have going for you towards the success of your stage exhibition of hypnotism. In other words, prestige and expectation are working in your favor, and, as a hypnotist, you know what this means for the successful induction of hypnosis.

Before we commence the hypnotism show, let's touch briefly upon a few essentials for being hypnotist, i.e., your appearance, your manner, your speech, and your presentation, viz.:

Bear in mind that when you hypnotize you are in close proximity with your subjects, thus your appearance is of great importance and must be acceptable to close scrutiny. To this end be neat and clean, and have your clothes immaculate. *In other words, look attractive.* The fictionized Svengali may have been a slovenly type, but that is no excuse for you to be such in this modern day-and-age.

As to your manner on stage, as a performer you have to present your suggestions so effectively that they will be unqualifiedly accepted to produce hypnosis. Do not boast or challenge, rather adopt the manner of the successful doctor. *Be quiet, reserved, dignified, direct, completely confident in knowing your work, and always entirely the master of the situation. And, above all, do not make your show a personal ego-trip. In other words, it is the purpose of your performance to entertain your audience not to flatter yourself. Further, as a professional stage hypnotist your purpose is to advance hypnotism as an art and increase knowledge of the science.*

In regards to your speech, speak clearly and well, and always with flawless English. *And know your hypnotism so throughly and your routine so perfectly that every word you say flows out and carries immediate conviction.*

As I have previously mentioned, as a stage hypnotist you have a dual delivery to get over: one to the audience and the other to your subjects. In addressing your audience your comments should be professional, good natured and to the point, *and presented much in the manner of an authoritive lecturer.* To your subjects, *your speech should be direct and positive.*

There is a certain knack to correctly giving suggestions that influence based upon principles which we have carefully considered in the first section of this book. The ability to apply these principles in action is something that you as a performing hypnotist must master. Generally speaking, your delivery should be such that while it may be quiet in tone, it instantly carries conviction and demands acceptance.

Having so equipped yourself, and armed with confidence in your ability both to entertain and hypnotize you are ready to present stage hypnotism, and just before you commence, *visualize in your mind with strong affirmation the mental picture and knowledge that your subjects and your audience will respond and react exactly as you plan they will. You are the leader and they must follow. There is powerful psychology at work here.*

Do not overlook this personal psychology, I have found it to be of the utmost importance to successful stage hypnotism.

You are now ready to step forward to the front of the stage (or whatever the performing situation may be) and further build-up your initial prestige with your opening lecture.

15
Opening
the Hypnotism Show

The opening lecture is very essential to the success of your hypnotic show. It sells you, it sells your potential subjects on the worthwhileness of hypnotism, and it secures volunteers to hypnotize from the audience. Learn and deliver your opening well -- *it has an important selling job to do.*

The average audience that the hypnotist faces is generally composed of three types of people: 1. The skeptics (those who do not believe in hypnotism and think its all a fake). 2. The credulous (those who believe in hypnotism, hold it in awe, and regard it as wonderful). 3. The witnesses (those who just come to see a show and hope that it will be amusing).

It is your job via your opening lecture, therefore, to even out these three types of spectators, and set them all on a common ground by convincing the skeptics that there really is a great deal to the subject of hypnotism, by fascinating yet further the believers (for here, in this group, you can expect to find some of your best subject material for the show), and arouse the interest of the casual showgoer so he will sit up ready to witness sparkling entertainment.

To meet these requirements, your opening lecture must be interesting, informative, illustrative, and stimulating . . . and do it all in a concise and entertaining manner so that audience interest is maintained as the spectators await the actual demonstration in hypnotism to commence.

The opening lecture which I will give you, as well as the body of the main hypnotism show described in the next chapter, are taken from my own performances as I have used same nationally and internationally. These will serve as a pattern for developing your own show. Full details of all patter, suggestion handling, etc. are presented to illustrate how the various waking suggestion experiments and hypnotic methods, *you have learned,* are applied and used in the hypnotism show for entertainment.

Let us now study the opening lecture.

Your stage (or whatever the performing situation may be) set with its customary semicircle of empty chairs, your introduction to the spectators completed, you approach your audience with a confident air and a friendly smile:

"Ladies and Gentlemen, with your kind attention I will present a number of scientific demonstrations in hypnotism. Before I begin, a few explanatory remarks will not be out of place.

"Hypnotism is now in a stage of advancement and achievement. While in the past it was often greeted with skepticism, today it is openly acclaimed, and is practiced by both medical doctors and university professors.

"As you are all undoubtedly aware, through the many popular articles on the subject in the news, hypnotism is now thoroughly recognized as a science throughout the entire civilized world.

"Now just what is hypnotism? Hypnotism, according to the latest psychological findings, has been defined as an extension of concentration ... in other words, it is the extraordinary power that ideas possess when they claim our complete attention. Such vitalized ideas are called suggestive ideas, and of such created what has become known as the power of suggestion.

"Let me, at this time, give you an example of this power of suggestion that we can all try together. It is an interesting little experiment that nicely illustrates the operation of this force which underlines hypnotism.

"For this experiment, everyone relax in your chairs, place your feet flat on the floor, and let your hands rest comfortably in your lap. And now. . . direct your attention towards me and towards this yellow, juicy, bitter lemon which I hold before you. It is such a sour, bitter lemon. I take this knife and cut into the lemon. Look at that sour juice as it drips to the floor. I am going to suck that sour, bitter juicy lemon. (Suck it audibly). The lemon is so bitter and sour. . . and as I suck it, notice how our mouths begin to fill with moisture and the saliva flows freely.

(Perform this example test with lemon in hand, and time your actions in accordance with your patter presentation.)

"We can all experience it. Our mouths fill with saliva as I suck the sour lemon. How does it psychologically operate? Well, first the lemon provides you with an idea -- an idea of something sour. This idea then becomes realized unconsciously in our minds, the salivary glands secrete, and our mouths fill with saliva. And here in this simple experiment, that everyone has felt, we observe the power of suggestion at work -- suggestion which is the basic of hypnotism.

"In a moment, I am going to request some volunteers to come forward to occupy these chairs, and to partipate in some interesting demonstrations in suggestion and hypnotism. I am sure you will find all of these experiments fascinating, and I assure you I shall treat everyone with the utmost courtesy and respect. I only request that those who come up on the stage be serious about experimenting with this wonderful state of mind, and that they will be willing to concentrate intently upon the suggestions offered. With such cooperation, together we shall achieve some most remarkable phenomena.

"Without further ado now, I invite you my friends -- yes, both ladies and gentlemen are welcomed -- to come forward and occupy these chairs as our hypnotism investigating committee. Come on up, let us experiment with hypnotism. Come up, come up now. That's it, come on up. No children please, only adults as these experiments require mature concentration."

So concludes the opening lecture as the volunteers commence coming forward to occupy the chairs. Let us pause briefly, and see where things stand now in relation to the show.

First, your opening lecture has acquainted your audience with yourself as a personality, and has placed hypnotism on its rightful pedestal as an accepted scientific fact.

Second, you have given a logical explanation for the phenomena, and further presented an actual demonstration of this power of suggestion, which everyone has felt. This lemon test is excellent, is graphic and splendidly shows, in a simple form, the operation of suggestion.

Third, you have requested adult volunteers to come forward to experiment with suggestion and hypnotism. Remember, you have not at anytime challenged any person to come forward and be hypnotized. Your statements clearly request that only those who are seriously interested and willing to cooperate come on stage as a hypnotism investigating committee. This handling is important as it gives you an excuse if later you have to send down any possible "wise guys" (occasionally there are some) from the stage. You have referred to hypnotism as a state of advanced concentration, so obviously if a person is not willing to cooperate and concentrate as you direct, no hypnosis is to be expected. You have "safe guarded" the success of your performance from the very start.

Statistics of hypnotic responsiveness show that one person out of five is a natural somnambulist -- in other words, is a really good hypnotic subject. In situations of prestige, such as at a performance, you can very likely increase that percentage, and there is also another factor at work in your favor for securing good subjects. Somnambulists have a tendency to attend hypnotic programs, and your advance announcements of such seems to attract them like a light does moths. Thus you may be sure that your audience will be well stocked with its full share of such persons.

As you appreciate, the trait of natural suggestibility is one of the major characteristics of a good hypnotic subject, so suggestion goes to work for you immediately when you ask for volunteers, i.e, there is the group of waiting chairs with their implied suggestion that they must be filled, and then there are your repeated suggestions, "Come up...come on up...come on up and volunteer." Over and over goes forth your request to come up and occupy those chairs; to come forward and experiment with hypnotism. It is a call that natural somnambulists simply cannot resist. So up they come as part of your committee, and hence are there to function as excellent subject with which you can demonstrate the phenomena of hypnosis.

As the volunteers comes forward, you greet each in turn with a firm handshake and a square look in the eyes. Right here you establish yourself as a warm human being, one who is to be respected and whose instructions are to be followed. Watch the volunteers as they take their seats. If friends come up together and start to talk to each other, rearrange their seating in the group, so they are seated amongst strangers. You must have complete attention.

With your committee now seated in a semicircle facing you; what have you here? Before you is a group of persons entirely unknown to yourself, and, as was the audience when you began your performance, this committee is composed of three types of individuals: (1) the natural somnambulists who are your really good subjects, (2) the genuinely interested who are persons who will cooperate with you and try their best to be hypnotized, (3) the skeptics who are persons with a "hypnotize me if you can" attitude.

Thus far your approach has been to level out the attitudes of your audience, you must now level out the attitudes of the committee. To do this, present the following comments which lays the success of the whole performance directly in their laps:

"Ladies and gentlemen of our investigating committe of hypnotism, I wish to thank you very much for coming forward and welcome each of you. As you undoubtedly appreciate, the ability to be hypnotized is in reality a skill that must be learned. And, as a skill, it naturally will require striving on your part for its accomplishment. That is why I ask your utmost efforts to concentrate well upon the suggestions which I will give you.

"Now, some persons seem to naturally possess this remarkable ability to enter hypnosis, while others have to practice to achieve it. It will be my purpose, during this performance, to help you pass into this amazing state of mind known as hypnosis."

By these remarks, you will note you have established hypnotism as a mental skill that takes ability to achieve. Thus, to resist your influence is to admit they haven't "what it takes." Nobody likes to admit this, so your skeptics are placed more on less on the spot; they had better follow along with you or else, in the eyes of the entire audience, they admit their inadequacy.

Remember this pattern in the forming of your entire successful hypnotism show, the things you do are never presented as a challenge of your powers over the subjects, rather, you are to be looked upon as an instructor, the teacher of a skill

110

that those qualified can achieve. *Your entire presentation is directed towards making the achieving of hypnosis seem an important accomplishment; the achieving of hypnosis must be "sold" as a worthwhile and desired goal. Both your committee members and the spectators must sense this.*

With your objective properly accomplished, your subjects will be in a frame of mind that far from wishing to resist hypnotic influence are actually anxious to see if they have the necessary skill to enter the state.

Several factors in the performing situation are working with you to help in fulfilling this objective. There is the audience which puts the subjects in a keyed-up mood – in a sense of feeling important in being part of the show before all the spectators; while, at the same time, they feel a little ill-at-ease and self conscious in being on stage.

Then, there are the curtains, the lights, the music, all the trappings of theatre which enter into the stage situation, as the case may be. *All such elements of the stage situation work directly with you towards the placing of the volunteers in a mood receptive to suggestion and expectant of being hypnotized.*

It will be found that even when a volunteer comes up on stage with skepticism, it isn't easy for him to continue to buck the tide of the stage situation, and many will soon slip into the path of least resistance; which path y o u a r e carefully paving along directly towards hypnosis.

There is definitely a pressure in the stage situation; you will feel it yourself. It is a sort of bond that unites the performer with the group attention of the audience. You, as the performer, are in the situation as the leader, and such spurs you along. Your subjects, on the other hand, are in the situation in submissive roles, and every last one of them feels it, as it lulls them into a welcomed retreat to enter deep hypnosis -- for such is what is expected of them to best fulfill the demands created in the immediate stage situation.

Make note of this psychology. Although the presentation of hypnotism on the stage may at first seem a difficult task, handled with intelligence it soon shapes itself up into a situation that you, as a hypnotist, will recognize as being most fertile for the production of hypnotic phenomena. At the same time, you will greatly appreciate the need for a thorough mastery of your subject and the careful routining of your demonstrations.

Before we proceed to a study of the body of the hypnotism show, let us consider some alternative opening approaches, viz.:

One handling includes in the opening lecture a waking suggestion experiment on the whole audience which culminates in bringing the more responsive subjects on stage. The procedure is to present an audience participation test for everyone to try directly following "the lemon experiment," in the lecture. You tie it in as follows, "...let me give you all another example of this power of suggestion. Everyone continue to relax in your chairs, as you have been doing. Now, close your eyes. Close them tightly together. Very tight, tight. Now, with your eyes closed, roll your eyes upwards, up under your closed eyelids, and look backwards, back into your very brain, as it were.

"Squeeze your eyelids together; they are becomming stuck. The lids are becoming stuck together. Stuck so tightly together that soon it will be impossible to open your eyes. They are stuck tightly together. That's it, keep looking backwards into your brain; your eyelids are stuck tightly together. They simply will not open no matter how hard you try. Try hard. Hard! They will not open no matter how hard you try!"

Watch your audience. Many spectators will struggle to open their eyes, but be unable to do so. After a few moments of fruitless attempts, suddenly clap your hands loudly and say, "All right, all right, it's all gone. You can open your eyes now. Open your eyes."

This test is an effective one to perform as the small muscles about the eyes are very susceptible to suggestion.

Having completed the "eyelid fastening experiment," you can invite those subjects who responded to it to come upon the stage for further demonstrations.

Another opening experiment that may be used on the entire audience is this variation of "The Hand Clasping Test." It was a favorite of the famous hypnotist, Konradi Leitner, who's handling I previously mentioned.

Following the point in your lecture where you wish to demonstrate an experiment in suggestion that the spectators may try, comment, "... response to suggestion occurs in direct ratio to a person's ability to concentrate. (There is good psychology in this line in associating the ability to concentrate with response to suggestion.) Let us all try this experiment together.

"Everyone raise your arms above your head. That's it. Lift your arms straight up into the air. Now turn your palms so they face each other, and spread your fingers wide apart. Now, place your hands together and interlock your fingers. Interlock your hands together tightly together. Squeeze tightly. Tight!"

As you give these directions, illustrate the procedure by raising your own hands above your head and interlocking your fingers tightly, as shown in Fig. 36.

Say, "Now turn your hands outward and upward ... that's it turn your hands right over so the palms are facing upwards and stretch out your arms straight above your head. Squeeze your fingers together tightly... very tightly. So tight. Keep your

Fig. 36

attention firmly concentrated on me. Your arms are becoming stiff. Push them up stiff...stiff. Your arms are becoming stiff and tense, and your hands are becoming tightly locked together. Your hands are stuck tight together, so tightly they simply will not come apart no matter how hard you try. Keep pushing your arms up stiff above your head. Your arms are stiff and your fingers are stuck together; your hands are glued together. See you cannot pull them apart. Try and pull them apart. You cannot! They simply will not come! They are stuck!"

Watch your audience carefully and observe their reactions. Some will take their hands apart, while others will find their hands stuck firmly and only be able to separate them after considerable effort. And there will be those amongst the audience who will be totally unable to take their hands apart. Address these people and invite them forward to the front of the stage to have their hands released.

Down the aisles they come, hands locked together over their heads. Each in turn you gaze in the eyes, and with a firm command, state, "It's all gone now. The influence is gone, and you can unlock your hands. Relax your arms. Relax your hands. Your hands are free!"

One by one you unlock the hands of each person, and invite them to come onto the stage to take part in further demonstration, if they wish. Having performed this interesting experiment, many will accept the invitation and you will shortly have your chairs filled with good potential subjects.

This method of fastening the hands together works excellently incorporating, as it does, both the suggestion factor as well as the physical one that when the fingers are so interlocked with the palms turned upward above the head, so long as the arms are held

113

stiff and pushing straight upward, as you instruct, it becomes muscularly difficult to realease the hands, and such serves as a reenforcement to the suggestions.

Some operators favor performing such tests upon the entire audience in suggestion as it helps them locate their best subjects. Other prefer leaving the audience alone and work only upon the subjects on stage. It is an arbitrary question as to which process is best, so use your own judgement.

You now have ample material with which to form an effective opening lecture. So prepared, you are ready to preceed on and study the performance of the main body of the hypnotism show.

16
The Hypnotism Show

Your volunteer subjects seated before you in a semicircle on stage, address the group as follows:

"On behalf of the entire audience, I wish to thank you, ladies and gentlemen, for so kindly volunteering. I will do my very best to make your stay here on stage interesting to both you and the audience, and above all of usefulness to yourself, for you are going to learn how to become masters of an ancient and wonderful art – the magic of the mind, HYPNOTISM."

Turn then and address the audience, "And ladies and gentlemen in the audience, kindly pardon my back as I must turn from time to time to address the committee during the hypnotic experiments you are about to witness. And, please, at the beginning of these experiments, kindly be as quiet as possible as such will assist these people on the stage in their efforts to properly concentrate. Later you may respond as you wish, but at first quietness will be a help and you will be extending to these friends upon the stage the same courtesy that you, yourself, would desire were you up here in their places."

First Group Experiment: The Hypnotic Mood Test

Turn sidewise to the audience and address the committee, "In our first experiment together, we shall produce what is called the hypnotic mood. It is a mood of rest, calmness, and relaxation. First, everyone sit back comfortably in your chair, place your feet flat on the floor, and rest your hands in your lap, each hand resting separately on each knee." See Fig. 37.

Fig. 37

"That's fine. Just adjust yourselves in your chairs so you will be perfectly comfortable. Now, everyone direct your complete attention towards me and pay close attention to every suggestion and idea which I will give you.

"Entering hypnosis is a skill, one might almost say it is a talent to be developed. The ability to enter hypnosis you can master with practice, and it is our purpose to practice together the development of this skill."

Watch your subjects carefully, and make certain that everyone gives you his (or her) undivided attention. This is most important: *be sure you have the complete attention of everyone in the committee exactly as you wish it before you proceed any further.* The subjects must be serious and absorbed in performing the hypnotic experiments together.

Then continue, "In order to be hypnotized you must be able to relax while at the same time you are concentrating intently, so we shall relax progressively, step by step. As I give you these thoughts to think about, concentrate like this:

"For example, if I should say that your arms are becoming heavy and that your hands are pressing down into your lap, think to yourself that your arms *are* getting heavy and that your hands are pressing down into your lap...and, as you do so, you will find that your arms and hands actually do feel heavier just as is being suggested.

"All right then, everyone think first of relaxing the muscles of your head, the scalp muscles. As you concentrate on relaxing these muscles, you will begin to feel a tingling sensation coming over your scalp. Now let your thoughts wander down over your face and relax the muscles of your face. Relax the muscles about your mouth, relax completely. Now relax the muscles of your neck and shoulders, down through to your chest. Relax every muscle of your body, right down through your thighs, your legs, down to your very feet. It feels so good to so perfectly relax your body. And, as you relax your body, your mind, too, begins to become relaxed and calm, and your eyes feel heavy. Your eyelids feel tired and heavy. Your eyes want to close. I will count now from one to three, and at the count of 'three' everyone close your eyes and relax completely. All ready! One...two...three. Close your eyes. That's it, everyone close their eyes down tightly."

Observe the subjects closely, and if anyone does not close their eyes point at them directly and say, "Close your eyes. Close them right down tightly." *Make sure all eyes of everyone in the committee are closed before you continue.*

"Now with your eyelids closed tight, roll your eyes back upward under the closed lids. Look back upwards toward the very center of your head. Roll your eyes back, and keep staring into your very brain. Your eyes are becoming stuck together, stuck so tightly together that they simply will not open try as hard as you will. Keep looking back into your brain, and try to open your eyes. Your eyes are stuck tightly closed, and you cannot open them try as hard as you will."

Here you are applying the "eyelid fastening test" which you have learned so well.

Your subjects will try in vain to open their tightly closed eyes. This is important as it convinces the group that some subtle influence is in operation over them. Continue on, "Forget about your eyes now, just rest quietly in blackness, and let that relaxation seep through every fibre of your being. It feels so good, so calming, so restful. And now you are beginning to get drowsy. Let yourself just drift along. You are becoming so sleepy and drowsy. I will count slowly from one to ten. With every count you will become drowsier and drowsier, and sleepier and sleepier. Let yourself go, let yourself just drift, drifting down to pleasant rest. *One... two...* you are getting so sleepy and drowsy. *Three... * you are becoming so relaxed. Let your head fall forward if you wish. Let every muscle of your body relax completely. *Four. . .five... six.* You are getting so calm and relaxed. So drowsy and sleepy. Let yourself just drift down to sleep, pleasant rest and sleep. *Seven...eight...nine.* Let yourself just drift down towards sleep and rest. Every muscle of your being is relaxed. *Ten!*

"Now pay close attention to every suggestion that I give you. As you rest there all calm and quiet, your mental processes are becoming intensified, becoming acute, so that you will find that you can concentrate easily and powerfully upon every suggestion I will give you. You will find that you can easily accomplish every demonstration, and follow perfectly every suggestion that I give you. You are resting calmly and quietly. Nothing will disturb or bother you, and you will find that you can concentrate intently upon every suggestion that I give you, and respond to every one."

Throughout all of your demonstrations on the stage, make generous use of your hands as you talk, performing graceful, rhythmic passes out from the sides of your head in gently sweeping motions towards your committee. See Fig. 38. These tend to hold the attention of both the subjects and the audience upon you.

"All right now, I shall count slowly from one to five. With every count you will begin to arouse yourself, and by the time I reach the count of five, you will be again all awake and alert. Ready, one, two, three...that's it, open your eyes now...four...all active and alert and ready to proceed to more advanced experiments. Five! Open your eyes everyone."

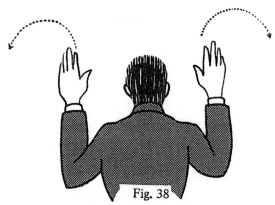

Fig. 38

This first experiment performed upon the comittee is most important to the success of your entire hypnotism show.

To the audience, it appears merely as an interesting beginning demonstration of relaxing the subjects and influencing them lightly. But actually you are accomplishing far more than this.

Notice that in presenting this beginning test, you do not mention that you intend to hypnotize, but rather that you will show the committe how to experience the hypnotic mood of relaxing while concentrating. Thus you avoid any possible challenge from any of the subjects resisting, and if one or two do not respond it makes little difference. But even though you are not deliberately hypnotizing, still every suggestion is designed to lead your subjects progressively into a light hypnotic state (such conditions are known as hypnodial states), first through relaxing of the body, then the eyelids closures and fastening, and finally through suggestions of drowisness and sleep.

As you perform this test, you can determine which of your subjects are the most responsive; likewise you can see which are the most resistive, and knowing the hypnotic effects you plan to present in the program, you can almost tell at this point which subjects would be best to use in the various tests as you have routined them.

Further, this initial test will have relaxed and calmed the group down from any tendencies of boisterousness, *and you have set in their minds suggestions leading to the ready acceptance and the following of every suggestion which you will give them to respond to each experiment perfectly.*

As a performer, you can see how very vital this first experiment is, so take your time with it, and get the group thoroughly relaxed and drowsy. Although some spectators in your audience seeing the subjects with their eyes closed and slumped down in their seats so relaxed will think that you have

118

hypnotized the entire group, actually very few will have gone into complete hypnosis up to this point, but such is unimportant. *The important thing is that you have increased the suggestbility responses of the committee members.*

Your hypnotism show is but beginning, yet through this very first step you have "stacked the cards" in your favor for the total success of your entire performance.

Now address the audience, "We are now ready for some psychological experiments demonstrating the power of suggestion in the waking state ... first, affecting the sense of balance. Who would like to be the first subject for this experiment?"

(You have learned how to perform experiments in waking suggestion in early chapters of this book. These tests are now being used in relation to stage show handling.)

First Individual Type Experiments: Posture Swaying Tests

THE FALLING BACKWARDS TEST. Turn and look over the committee, select a subject who followed your suggestions well in the first group experiment so you can feel certain he will respond positively to this test. *This is your first individual demonstration of hypnotic effect, and it is important to your performing prestige that it succeeds.*

Always select a responsive male subject for this test. Have him step forward and ask him in a friendly fashion if he is willing to try an experiment in suggestion. When he agrees, follow on with your presentation, "All right then. Stand facing me here in the center of the stage with your feet side by side together. That is fine. Now in this experiment we are going to demonstrate how thoughts can actually influence the sense of balance as you concentrate. In a moment, I will stand behind you, and you will feel an impulse to fall right over backwards. Now, have no fear of falling, as I will be right behind you and will catch you. All ready?"

As you give these directions, look him steadily in the eye, and in a soft confidential manner request him to keep his mind intent on the ideas you will give him. When his eyes become fixed and steady on yours, compliment him by saying, "Fine, you concentrate splendidly." Now tell him to close his eyes and relax his body. Place your hand on his shoulder moving him backward and forward a bit to make certain that he is properly relaxed; tell him to imagine himself as a plank of wood hinged to the floor, and that he can sway easily in either direction backward or forwards, then say:

"All ready now, I will step behind you, and you will feel an impulse pulling you right over backwards toward me. Have no fear of falling; I will catch you. All ready now, eyes closed, relax and concentrate."

Then softly, to the subject confidentially, say, "Let yourself go and don't resist. Let yourself come right back towards me as you concentrate on the influence which will pull you right over backwards."

These intimate "asides" spoken quietly and personally to the subject are important to your stage handling of the hypnotism entertainment. The audience hears only the major portions of your comments which describe and explain each experiment, but the subject receives full benefit of your confidence which makes him feel responsible to concentrate well and respond successfully to each test. Further, such handling increases the direct influence of your suggestions. This is professional stage hypnotism technique that is frequently employed in diversified ways.

Now step behind your subject, touch him lightly on the back of his head so he will know that you are standing behind him, and begin suggesting, "You will feel an impulse pulling you right over backwards. Concentrate your thoughts on falling over backwards. Falling backwards. You are falling back, back, right over backwards. Have no fear of falling, I will catch you."

As you give these suggestions, draw your hands back from his body as shown in Fig. 39. To the spectators, it appears exactly as if some mysterious "force" from your hands were pulling him right over backwards. Soon the subject will fall directly backward into your arms. You catch him and at once assist him to regain his balance.

Fig. 39

Here is an important piece of business in handling this test. If you were to stand behind your subject and commence at once your drawing passes, and he did not fall, then you are "on the spot" as having failed in your very first individual test. This seldom happens but it is not impossible, and a failure at this commencing point in your show is very bad indeed. To safeguard the operation, as you begin your suggestions of falling backwards, do not stay directly behind the subject but rather step to his side momentarily, cross your arms unconcernedly. Then, *as he starts to fall in response to the suggestions,* step behind him and commence your mysterious pulling passes, catching him as he falls.

It is the little things like this that make the stage hypnotist the master of each situation, as observed in this subtlety: from the audience's point-of-view you have not even started your experiment until such time as you step behind the subject and begin the passes that appear to draw him over backward. Also, it gives you a chance to judge the responses of your subject. Should it appear that he is not relaxing sufficiently or is resisting your suggestions, you can stop the proceeding before going any further and explain to him the importance of his concentrating, not resisting, and letting himself respond freely. Or, should he by some chance absolutely refuse to respond (this is very rarely the case since you have had a good opportunity to select a suitable subject from the group) you can even send him back to his seat, and select another subject for the experiment.

This principle of basically conducting two shows at the same time, one for the audience and the other for the subject or subjects is an important factor to keep in mind in relation to your successful staging of the hypnotism show. I have gone into this matter at some length in connection with this test as I want you to have these insights of expert performance.

Your first individual subject having fallen backwards and again returned to his seat, you can say to him, "It felt just like a force of some kind pulling you right over backward, didn't it?" The subject will confirm. Here you have further established the audience's impression that you actually drew the subject over through the application of some special "force," and have also prepared the other subjects in the group to respond accordingly. *Throughout the hypnotism show, it is well to maintain this pattern, letting each successful experiment lead directly on to other successful experiments.*

Now select another male subject and repeat "The Falling Backward Test." Next perform it with a girl. The use of a young lady adds variety and charm to the repeated tests.

Next take another male subject and draw him over backwards.

After he responds, apparently as an afterthought hold on to him, and keep him beside you as you explain to the audience, "Occasionally I have heard the comment from people witnessing these experiments that a person tends naturally to fall over backwards. Such is not true, and to prove it, let us reverse the expériemnt and try it -- this time falling forwards. You see, the influence operates in any direction, backward, forward, or to the sides."

THE FALLING FORWARD TEST. Using the same subject who has been standing beside you, perform this experiment. Have him take a position before you with his feet together, tell him to keep his eyes open this time and stare directly into your right eye, while you, in turn, gaze into his. Then lift your hands to positions on opposite sides of his head, and suggest:

"You will begin to feel an impulse this time to fall forward... you are swaying forwards right over towards me. Let yourself come. I will catch you. You are falling forwards, Forward. Right over forward!"

As you give these suggestions, draw your hands in passes away from him, and slowly draw your body backward and downward. See Fig. 40. The subject will follow your eyes, and as you draw back will sway forward, and topple right over in your arms. Catch him, and help him to regain his balance.

Fig. 40

THE SITTING TEST. Since the subject you have been using has proved himself responsive to your suggestions, retain him for the performance of this experiment which immediately follows the foregoing.

Have a chair brought center stage, and request the subject to be seated. Then address both the subject and the entire committee:

"Rather than performing these, what psychologists call posture sway experiments upon each of you individually, we will try an experiment all together. So watch this next text very closely; then, in a moment, we will all perform it together."

Turn to the seated subject and ask that he rise and stand directly in front of his chair with his feet together, and explain, "In this experiment, you will feel an impulse not only pulling you over backwards, but your knees will come forward, and you will sit right back down in that chair."

Then ask the subject to close his eyes, and commence making passess -- pushing out from the sides of your face in towards him, as you suggest, "All ready you begin to feel an impulse pulling you over backward. You are going to fall right back, your knees are bending, and you are going to sit right back down in that chair. Sit down in the chair. Sit down. You are swaying backwards, sitting down. Sit down. Sit down. Sit down!" Bend in close to the subject as you give these suggestions, as shown in Fig. 41. He will shortly sway backwards and suddenly sit down in the chair with a thump! Thank him for his fine concentration, and allow him to return to the group.

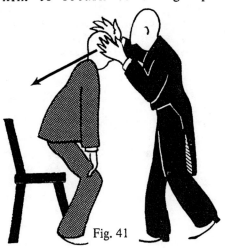
Fig. 41

Second Group Experiment: The Committee Sitting Test

Turn and address the committee, "All right now, let us all try that experiment together as a group. Everyone stand up right in front of their chair. That's fine. Place your feet together, and let your hands relax at your sides. Now, one thing is very important, be sure your chair is right behind you.

123

"All right everyone, stand relaxed directly in front of your chair. Now there is a large group performing this experiment, so obviously I cannot work individually with each of you, but you can work individually with me. So forget all about the others near you. Forget all about the audience. Consider this an experiment just between you and me. All right now, close your eyes."

In performing this test, your back is towards the audience and you are facing the committee. Commence making passes out from the sides of your head in large sweeping motions pushing toward the group, and suggest, "In a moment, you will begin to feel a swaying impulse to fall right over backward and sit down in your chairs. All ready, you begin to feel that swaying sensation. Your are going over backwards, losing your balance and are falling back, back, backwards. Let yourself go right along with it. You are swaying back, back, backwards. Your knees are coming forward, you are falling backwards, and sitting right down in your chairs. Sit down. Sit down in your chair. Sit down!"

By this time many of the committee will have started to sway, and as you continue your suggestions some one or two persons will suddenly fall back in their seat with a thump. And this "thump" of the first subjects falling will start the others ... and down they go, falling back with thuds into their seats, until almost everyone in the group finds himself seated. Possibly one or two subjects will still be left standing. If so, merely request them to open their eyes and have a seat, as you graciously gesture and explain that next time you hope they will be able to concentrate better. They take their seat, feeling a little foolish at finding themselves the only ones standing while all the rest are seated. You immediately turn to the audience and comment:

"Ladies and gentlemen, you see here an interesting example of personal variability in response to suggestion. Some of the subjects felt the effects almost immediately, other not quite so rapidly, and some few not at all. Why is this? The reason lies mainly in the degree of the concentration on the suggestions by the individual person."

Turn now so you are facing halfway towards your subjects so they can get the full benefit of your next remarks, "You see, a person must concentrate to their very utmost if they are to acquire this skill of mastering their body with their mind."

In this forceful statement, you have again hammered home the necessity of full attention and concentration, and motivated the subjects yet further to try even harder in the experiments yet to follow.

You have made a big production out of this series of posture swaying experiments as a sensational opening for your show, and this group sitting test last performed is exceedingly important for observing the reactions of your subjects. *Note in what order they fall back in their chairs.* The ones who first respond (and respond the best) are the subjects you are going to especially select for the next effective tests.

Second Type Individual Experiments: Muscular Catalepsy

THE HANDS FASTENING TEST. This classic experiment in suggestion is used in the hypnotism show, in this manner, as a transition experiment on to more advanced demonstrations.

Address the audience, "We will try some more advanced experiments in the power of suggestion, this time influencing the muscles of the body."

Turn to your committee, and point to the person in the group who fell back into his chair the most rapidly in the preceding test, and ask, "Will you kindly assist me?"

The subject comes forward and takes a position near the front of the stage. He stands sidewise to the audience facing you, as you state, "We are now going to lock your hands together by the power of suggestion so firmly that they will not come apart no matter how hard you try to separate them."

Then say to the committee, "Everyone please watch this experiment carefully as, in just a few moments, we will all try this test together at the same time."

As I have previously commented, you will notice how the routining of these tests are psychologically handled, *so that one demonstration sells the one next to follow.* In this instance, your subject here feels that he is setting an example for the group, and hence feels responsible that he must do a good job in performing the experiment. The group, on the other hand, becomes expectant of shortly trying the test themselves and look forward to it, and when they see its success on the one subject, they are *set* to expect it to work upon themselves.

Tell your subject out in front to look directly into your right eye, as you gaze back into his. Watch his eyes closely, if they wander in the slightest, command him to keep them firmly fixed on yours, and when they become set, compliment him softly, "Splendid, you concentrate excellently."

Now suggest loudly, "All right, raise up your hands, hold your arms straight out towards me and interlock your fingers in this manner." Illustrate the procedure by interlocking you own fingers and holding your hands outstretched in front of yourself, continue, "That's it. Now press your hands tightly together. Squeeze them together with all of your might. Squeeze them tight, tighter, tighter! Your hands are stuck tightly together now."

Continue illustrating the process by pressing your own hands tightly together right along with the subject, as shown in Fig. 42. Then, as you proceed, seperate your hands and make gentle passes down his arms from the elbows to the hands. Squeeze his arm muscles here and there, as you suggest:

"Your hands are tense and tight. All of your muscles are tense and tight." Take his hands in yours and press them tighter together as you say, "Your hands are becoming locked together so tightly that they simply will not come apart, no matter how hard you try. I will count from one to three, and at the count of 'three,' you will find you cannot pull your hands apart no matter how hard you try. Your hands are locked tight, tight together."

Keep the subject's eyes firmly fixed upon your own as you slowly back away from him, as you count, "One ... two ... three!" Then increase the force and tempo of your suggestions, saying very positively, "Your hands are locked fast together. They won't come apart no matter how hard you pull on them. Pull on them! Pull on them with all of your mind, but they won't come apart! They are stuck! They won't come apart no matter how hard you try! Pull! Pull! Pull with all of your might!"

Fig. 42

The subject will pull and struggle to separate his locked hands, but they resist all his efforts. Some subjects will try to pull their hands apart so violently they actually become "red in the face." Keep your eyes intently on the subject as he starts to pull on his hands, but after you see that they are powerfully locked together, you can turn your gaze away and leave him entirely on his own. It is a very effective test.

After the subject has struggled for a time, approach him and say, "All right now. When I snap my fingers beside your ear, your hands will instantly come right apart. All ready now."

Snap your fingers, and his hands instantly separate. Thank the subject, and have him return to his seat as you address the group.

Third Group Experiments:
The Hand Locking Test on the Committee

"Everyone in the committee now give me your complete attention. We are all going to try together the hand locking experiment you have just witnessed. This test is an achievement in concentration; the more powerfully you can concentrate, the better it will succeed ... so let's all try hard for one hundred percent results.

"Everyone ready? Good. Sit back in your chairs and place your hands in your lap, and look directly at me. Now everyone push your arms out towards me and make them stiff and rigid. That's fine. Now interlock your fingers in this manner"

Demonstrate by interlocking your own fingers to show them how to do it. Continue, "Very good. Keep pushing your arms right out straight in front of you, and squeeze your hands tightly together. Keep your eyes fixed on mine, and concentrate on your arms and hands becoming stiff and rigid with your fingers locked together."

Run your eyes rapidly from one end of the committee to the other, then as you start your actual suggestions, focus your gaze at a point about a foot above the head of the central subject in the group, and direct your suggestions forcefully towards that spot. This bit of technique, as was previously mentioned, seems to produce an effect of abstraction that holds the attention of the entire group more firmly than if you shift your gaze constantly about from one person to another. Having the attention of all the subjects on you, commence your "hand locking suggestions," (use the same suggestion formula for this in working with the group that you did in working with the solo subject), becoming more and more forceful as you proceed, and climaxing your suggestions with:

"I will count now from one to three, and at the count of 'three' your hands will be locked so firmly together they won't come apart no matter how hard you try! One ... two ... THREE! Your hands are locked tight. They won't come apart. Pull on them with all your might! They won't come apart, they are locked tightly together, tight, tight together! Pull on them. PULL! PULL! PULL!"

As you give these suggestions in group experience, use the familiar sweeping passes out from the sides of your head in towards the committee as you have in all the group tests; these passes assist greatly in holding the attention of everyone riveted towards you.

The subjects will find their hands locked together in response to your suggestions. Struggle as they will, they cannot separate their hands. You quickly pass around the committee of subjects, and one by one, release their hands with a snapping of your fingers, and the suggestion, "All right, all right. It's all gone now. Relax and take your hands apart."

I always regard the completion of this group "hand locking test" as sort of a milestone in the hypnotism show. Your subjects in responding to it will have made themselves responsive to further experiments in suggestion, also by keeping tabs of the various subjects in the group you can accurately select those best for subsequent tests.

Concentrate your attention now on this next experiment with the committee members.

Fourth Group Experiment:
Fingertip Sticking and Fingertip Missing

This experiment with the group follows naturally the foregoing one. Your show is beginning to take on tempo and speed, *so keep the pace going.* Ask the committee to raise up their hands in front of themselves and place the tips of their forefingers together, as shown in Fig. 43. Tell them to center their eyes on their touching fingertips, and to press them firmly together.

Suggest, "Concentrate on your touching fingertips. Your fingertips are becoming stuck tightly together just like your hands were before. They are stuck tight together; they are glued to each other. They are glued tight together, and you cannot get them apart. Try hard to pull them apart, but they will not separate no matter how hard you pull." Give your suggestion for this test in a rapid, forceful manner. It was amazing to the spectators to see the subjects unable to unlock their hands, but this test making it impossible to pull their fingertips apart is positively astonishing!

After the members of the committee have struggled to separate their fingertips for a few moments, say, "All right, everyone look at me. Forget about your fingers. They will come apart now." Clap your hands, and everyones' fingertips separate.

You will find, as you get your performance rolling and your subjects under control, that you can increase the speed of performing each test. Less and less "suggestive formula" need be employed, and you can become more and more commanding in the giving of your suggestions. Proceed immediately from the foregoing test into this one:

"Now everyone hold your fingertips about six inches apart. Those fingers are getting so nervous that you simply cannot make them meet. No matter how hard you try, you cannot make them meet. Those fingertips simply will not meet. Try and bring the tips together. See how they miss touching each other every time. See how they miss, how nervous they are. They simply will not meet. Try to touch them together but it is impossible, they miss every time. Try hard. It is impossible to make them touch!" See

Fig. 44.

As you give these suggestions, emphasize the action by holding your own fingertips apart and making them miss everytime you approach the tips together. When the whole committee is excitedly striving in vain to make their fingertips touch, suddenly clap your hands, and say, "All right. All right. It's all gone. Your fingertips will meet now!"

Further Waking Suggestion Experiments With Individual Subjects

You can now perform some sensational tests in waking suggestion using your best subject in the group, viz.:
HEAVY WATER - SHAKY POURING - BITTER WATER - THE MOUSE ON THE FLOOR. This experiment makes use of "the confusion technique," which was previously discussed. Each suggestion is heaped upon the subject in rapid succession. Each test leads directly from one to the other with scarcely a pause between them. Your manner is aggressive, and the subject is given little time to think as you forcefully pile suggestion upon suggestion and the experienced responses lead to increased suggestibity. This test (or combination of tests) is a masterpiece and was used by the famous Danish hypnotist, DeWaldoza as a climax to his program.

For this experiment, bring forward a subject who has proved responsive to your suggestions. Have him sit in a chair near the center of the stage as you gaze in his eyes, and suggest that he will respond positively to every suggestion you give him. When his eyes take on that intense fascinated look which you will have come to associate with experiments in waking suggestion, tell him to go over to the side of the stage to a table on which is a glass and pitcher of water. Ask him to lift up the glass in one hand and the pitcher in the other. See Fig. 45.

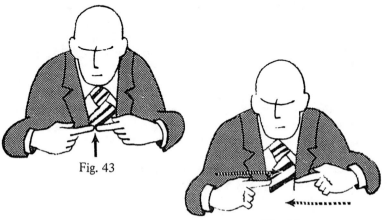

Fig. 43

Fig. 44

129

Fig. 45

The subject does this, and you tell him to replace the glass and pitcher on the table. Request him to retain his grip tightly upon these objects and to concentrate on your suggestions, as you say, "Now that glass and pitcher of water are becoming very heavy. So very heavy that they are stuck to the table. You cannot lift them no matter how hard you try. Try hard to lift them, but you cannot!"

The subject struggles to lift the objects from the table but is unable to do so.

While he is tugging, you approach him and without a pause continue right on with further suggestions, "All right now, you can lift the pitcher and the glass. Lift them right up, and pour the water from the pitcher into the glass."

The subject does as you directed, and you continue, "Say, look at your hands ... look at your hands, they are getting shaky. Your hands are beginning to shake ... your hands are getting nervous. You are shaking so much that the water is spilling about everyplace. You cannot control your shaking ... the water is spilling everyplace."

As you present these suggestions, stand in close beside your subject, and make your own motions jerky and nervous -- shaking your hands spasmodically. And continue to give your suggestion in this test in a short, jerky manner in keeping with your gestures of nervous shaking.

The subject will follow right along with you; his hands will begin to shake, and the more he shakes the more he shakes, and he will soon be spilling water every which way. Your suggestions at this point are directed not so much at him apparently as at the offending objects themselves, as you continue, "Why are you so nervous? What is the matter with those objects? Why can't you control them? What is the matter, you are spilling water all over yourself."

After the subject has spilled a good portion of the water in his pouring efforts, calm him with, "All right now. You're all calm now. Take the pitcher and fill the glass of water. That's it. See, it's easy now. Take the glass of water back to your chair, and have a seat."

You move with your subject and stand in front of him at his chair. Stand a bit to the right side so as not to mask the view of the audience from the action. Tell the subject to take a sip of the water, and ask him how it tastes? He will say okay. Then catch his eye, and suggest forcefully:

"That water no longer tastes good. It is old and stagnant. It is putrid water...the kind with the green scum on top. It reeks and smells. How awful it tastes. You hate it! Take a sip of that vile, scummy water. Just a little sip, for it will taste so bitter you will spit it out right away!"

Force the subject to take a sip of the water, and instantly suggest, "How awful it tastes. It is so bitter. Spit out that water. Spit it out!" The subject will wrinkle up his nose, go through a wonderful pantomine of disgust, and end up by violently spitting out the water, much to the delight of the audience.

Immediately catch his eye again, and tell him, "All right now, that bad taste is all gone. It's all gone. The taste is now all sweet and good."

Note how you are piling suggestion upon suggestions, each response leads to a further response as one test in suggestion dovetails into the next in this confusion technique. The mind of the subject is not allowed time to analyse things or be critical. The suggestions are positive and must be accepted.

Take the glass from the subject, point to an imaginary spot in the air, and continue right on, "Look up there. See that bright light ...way out there. See it! Look at it!"

The subject stares and you continue, "Say that light is beginning to grow larger. It is getting closer to us." Gesture with your hands as though something were passing through the air and coming right up onto the stage. Then point to the floor at the subject's feet, as you say,

"Here it is on the floor. Look, it isn't a light at all, IT'S A MOUSE! It's running all about."

Make your suggestions with mounting excitement, as you say, "It's a mouse, and it's running up your leg! Get it out! Get it out!" Suddenly bend over, move your fingers rapidly in a zigzag low to the stage as though you were following the running course of the mouse, and plunge your right hand up the cuff of his pant leg, as you say excitely, "Get it out! Get it out! Get it out!"

The subject will jump about, shaking his leg trying to rid himself of the imaginary mouse. You bring a chair forward, tell him to get up on it to get away from the mouse. And when the action is at its pitch, clap your hands and suggest, "All right. Everything is all right now. It's all gone." You thus end the experiment rapidly right at its climax. The subject will shake his head in bewilderment. You thank him, and he returns to his seat in the committee.

You have observed in this progressive experiment in waking suggestion a very significant type of hypnotic phenomena, for you have produced an hallucination in the waking state. It is little wonder that some psychologists refer to such experiments as waking hypnosis. Indeed, as you progress upwards towards more advanced demonstrations in waking suggestion, an overlapping seems to occur and what began as waking suggestions (in normal consciousness) becomes hypnosis (altered consciousness).

You are now ready to present the induction of hypnosis upon the stage.

Turn and address the audience, "Thus far, ladies and gentlemen, you have witnessed demonstrations in suggestion in what is called the wakeful state of mind. Let us now experiment with the actual induction of hypnosis. Who would like to volunteer to be the first subject?"

Inducing the Hypnotic Trance

Point to someone in the committee that you feel would respond well to hypnosis; if you wish, choose a subject, who, while responsive, has been somewhat sluggish in reacting to waking tests. In every committee you are bound to note such persons who are on the lethargic side, and this is a good chance to put one to work. Bring the subject forward and have him sit in a chair, center stage, with his right side towards the spectators. You take a position in front of the subject ready to hypnotize. Begin by asking the subject a few questions:

"Have you ever been hypnotized? Are you perfectly willing to be hypnotized?" Get his answers, and then explain, "Now, hypnosis is a condition very closely resembling sleep. The major difference is this however: if I were to appoach you while you slept and were to speak to you, you would be disturbed and might awaken. Right? However, when you are hypnotized, I can talk to you all that time and you will not be disturbed, but will go right on sleeping in hypnosis. You see, your mental state in hypnosis is almost exactly the same as when a person walks in their sleep. See what I mean?"

Turn to the committee and say, "Now everyone please observe very closely this experiment, for just soon as it is completed, we will all try hypnotism together." You are establishing

132

prehypnotic suggestions which will later assist in hypnotizing the entire group.

Directly facing your subject, bend towards him slightly and hypnotize him. I use my "progressive method," which you have learned. On the stage you can usually condense it and proceed quite rapidly, as you say, "Look me directly in the eye, the right one. Keep your gaze fixed upon my eye. Your eyes are becoming riveted to mine, and already your eyelids are beginning to get heavy. Your eyes are beginning to burn, you want to close them. But your cannot close them yet, for they are fastened intently upon my eyes. But now I will count slowly from one to ten, and with every count your eyes will become heavier and heavier, until by the time I reach ten, before, you will close those tired eyes. Ready, one...two. Your eyes are so tired. So tired. Close those tired eyes. Three...four. Close your tired eyes. Get that pleasant relief. Five...six...seven. That's it, close those tired eyes. How good it does feel to close those tired eyes. Close them tight. Tight. Eight. Eyes all closed. Nine... TEN. Now your eyes are becoming stuck tightly together."

At this point in the induction, you lean forward and make contact passes gently over his eyes, rubbing outward from the root of the nose toward the temples, and suggest, "Your eyes are stuck so tightly together now that they simply will not open. See how they stick together!"

The subject struggles to open his eyes, but fails. You follow right on, "All right, forget all about your eyes now, and go sound to sleep. Go deep asleep. Deep, deep asleep."

Step to the rear of the subject, stroke his forehead a few times and then stroke the back of his head from the crown down to the nape of his neck. See Fig. 46. Continue to suggest, "You are going down deep, deep asleep. Go sound to sleep!"

Watch the subject's breathing, and as it deepens, suggest, "Your breaths are coming in deeper and deeper. Breathe deep and free, and every breath you take is sending you down deeper and deeper to sleep." Then place your left hand on his left shoulder and press downward firmly so that his body tends to slump down in his chair. At the same time, with your right hand, tilt his head forward on his chest, as shown in Fig. 47.

Continue, "Everything is becoming far, far away to you. You are going deep, deeply to sleep." Then step to the front of your subject, and, as you suggest that every muscles in his entire body is relaxed and that he is asleep, pick up one of his hands and let it drop limply to his side. Let his other hand drop likewise. Put your hand on the back of the subject's neck and push his head down so that it rests on his knees. See Fig. 48.

Again pick up the subject's dangling arms and let them drop rag-like to his sides. Then flop his arms about loosely. This

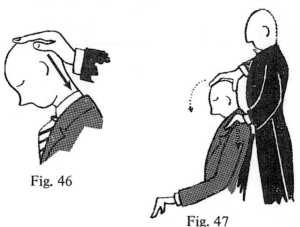

Fig. 46

Fig. 47

always causes a rise from the audience, as you address them, "You will note, ladies and gentlemen, that perfect relaxation. And right here you are observing an important aspect of hypnosis -- the complete relaxation it produces. Indeed, some say that the relaxation produced in hypnosis is so great that in ten minutes of the hypnotic trance a person can obtain as much rest as the average person does in a full night's sleep. And yet, a mere suggestion and that relaxation can instantly change to catalepsy."

Pick up the subject's right hand and stretch it out straight from his shoulder as you suggest to the hypnotic, "Your arm and hand are becoming stiff, STIFF! Hold it out straight and stiff. "You will feel the muscles of the subject's arm contract, you can let go of his hand, and the arm remains outstretched in the air, as you suggest, "That arm is becoming so stiff and rigid that you cannot bend it no matter how hard you try. Try to bend it, but you cannot!"

The subject will try to bend it, but the arm resists all of his efforts and remains stiff. Then pick up his left arm and hold it outstretched beside the other one, and say loudly, "STIFF!" That arm, also, becomes stiff and rigid. Both of the subject's arms are now outstretched in the air, as shown in Fig. 49.

Again speak to the audience, "Now watch the instant return to complete relaxation."

Again address the subject, "The moment I reach the count of 'three' your arms will instantly relax and will fall limply to your sides, and the moment they hit your sides they will send you down deeper and deeper into the very deepest sleep. (Note compounding of hypnotic suggestions again.) All ready, when I reach the count of three, your arms will instantly relax and fall like rags to your sides."

Gently touch the sides of the subject's thighs as you give the

134

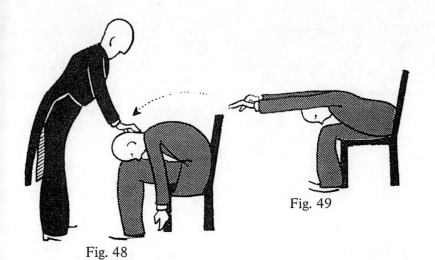

Fig. 49

Fig. 48

above suggestions, then count slowly, "One...two...THREE."
Instantly his arms will collapse and drop limply to his sides.
Again flop his arms about illustrating the complete relaxation
produced in hypnosis, then address the audience:

"Ladies and gentlemen, this hypnotized man could sleep – just
as you see him here -- in the hypnotic trance for a number of
hours, but time passes rapidly, so let's remove the state at once.
Now, the one thing most people seem to fear about hypnotism
appears to be the removal of the trance. It is a fear without basis
in fact however, and there is no danger whatsoever if it is handles
correctly. Note how gently and easily the subject awakens."

Now address the subject, "You have been having a most pleasant sleep in hypnosis, and it has done you a great deal of good,
but now the time is coming to awaken. So get ready to wake up.
I will count slowly from one to five -- with every count you will
gradually awaken, and by the time I reach 'five' be wide, wide
awake and feeling fine. All ready. One... two... three... four..
. FIVE. That's it. Wake up. . . wide awake and just feeling fine."

The subject awakens, looks about, and stretches. You thank
him and invite the audience to give him a round of applause, and
he returns to his seat in the committee.

*In performing on the stage, always hypnotize as rapidly as you
can.* A long drawn-out technique of hypnotizing is scarcely very
entertaining to the audience. Fortunately, the stage situation
makes it possible to often hypnotize in a matter of seconds.
Some subjects will go into hypnosis almost instantly the moment
they close their eyes, and you have but to command, "Sleep!"
and proceed directly into the arm relaxation and catalepsy test.
This rapidity of trance induction in stage entertainments of
hypnotism is one of the marvels that thrills the audience.

Sixth Group Experiment:
Mass Hypnotizing of the Entire Committee

Face your committee and say, "All right everyone, let's all try the experiment of entering hypnosis together. You have come on stage for the purpose of being hypnotized, so here is your chance to enter this very interesting state. You will find it most pleasant, so everyone give it your undivided attention and concentrate to the utmost, and I will likewise do my very best to help you.

"All ready, seat yourselves back comfortably in your chairs, place your feet flat on the floor, and let your hands rest in your lap. That's right, let one hand rest on each knee, so your fingers do not touch. Now each of you direct your gaze fixedly towards me, and – all together – when I say inhale, inhale a deep breath. Hold it, and then exhale as I direct. Everyone now, *inhale.*"

Gesture towards the committee as you give the suggestions to the group by making hypnotic passes with your hands outstretched above your head and move them downward towards your sides as you inhale along with the subjects, and then move them upwards as you exhale. See Fig. 50.

Fig. 50

Continue, "Hold it . . . hold that breath. Hold it and now exhale slowly. Good. Now once again . . . Inhale . . . hold it . . . and exhale. And for a thrid and last time. Inhale deeply . . . hold the breath . . . now exhale.

"How pleasant and relaxed that makes you feel, and as you look directly at me, already you begin to feel a calmness creeping over you, a pleasant sensation of warmth is growing all about you, and your eyes begin to feel heavy and tired. They want to close. All right, I will count slowly from one to ten, and with every count they will slowly close more and more, so by the time I reach 'ten' or before, close your eyelids right down tight together and shut out the light. Ready. One . . . two . . . three . . . four . . . eyes closing all down tight. Five . . . six . . . seven. Close those tired eyes and let them rest. Eight . . . nine . . . TEN. Eyes all close together shutting out the light. Eyes all closed tight!"

Glance over the entire committee; all subjects' eyes should be closed. If any are not, point to such persons and request them to close their eyes, then continue, "It feels so good to close those tired eyes. So good, and they are so tightly closed that they are getting all stuck together, and you cannot open them. The eyes are stuck and they will not open. See how they stick."

In working with the entire committee, don't make an issue of this, but rather continue immediately on, "Forget all about your eyes now and go to sleep. Go sound to sleep. Sleep Sleepy sleep. You are going down deep, deep asleep. Go sound to sleep."

By now many subjects will be nodding and breathing deeply, so starting at the left end of the group, go to each in turn and make a few contact passes on their foreheads out from the root of the nose towards the temples as you pass along, and suggest directly into the ear of each, "That's right. . . go to sleep now. You are concentrating splendidly. Go sound to sleep. Nothing will bother you. Just go sound, sound to sleep." And push each subject's head forward onto their chest on through the entire group. Work rapidly, then return to stage center and suggest, "Nothing will bother you at all. You are all sleeping pleasantly and deeply. Go deeper and deeper to sleep. You are breathing deep and freely, deep and freely, and every breath you take is sending you on down deeper and deeper to sleep. (Note once again how in this deep breathing suggestion you are *compounding suggestions* in which the response to one suggestion increases the force of another, it is professional technique for inducing hypnosis.) Go deep, deep asleep. Sound asleep."

Look your committee of subjects carefully over at this point, *for here is an opportunity to diplomatically get rid of those persons who are not responding as they should, and you do not wish to retain on the stage.* If any subjects are proving undesirable, quietly approach them, and with your finger to your lips, whisper, "Thank you very much for volunteering but since you find it difficult to concentrate on the stage I believe you will most enjoy watching the show from the audience. Please walk down very quietly so as not to disturb any of the subjects concentrating in hypnosis.

There is good psychology in this handling as it removes unwanted subjects at a time in the show when the audience's attention is centered on watching the subjects who are responding, also your words in dismissing unwanted subjects is picked up inconspicuously by those who are concentrating correctly and motivates them to yet more effective efforts. Dismissal of unwanted subjects at this time is very logical as it is obvious that you would not wish to retain any wakeful persons who might possibly disturb the hypnotized subjects.

GROUP HAND RAISING TEST. Continue on with your suggestions, "Now, in a moment, you will begin to feel a sort of tingling sensation coming into your fingertips. It will be a pleasant tingle, and you can feel it passing up your arms. It makes your hands restless in your lap. Your hands are getting lighter and lighter; they are beginning to raise up from your lap. Your hands are raising up. Hands lifting, raising right up into the air. Raise them up. All hands coming up. UP! Hold them outstretched directly out in front of yourself."

Observe your committee closely. Hands will begin to slowly lift up from the laps of subjects throughout the group. Some will respond more rapidly than other; as long as you have a good showing you need not bother to take the time to make every subject respond. A good two-thrids of the committee with their hands up in the air is sufficient. See Fig. 51.

Fig. 51

Spot the five subjects who raised their hands up first in the group. Walk over to the one nearest you, touch him lightly on the head, and command, "Rise up out of your chair and walk!" Take him by the hand and get him started. As soon as he is on his feet and walking, pass on to each of the remaining selected subjects and repeat the test. The effect of the five subjects slowly walking across the stage, zombie fashion, with their arms stretched out in front of them, is weird and startling.

Keep your eyes on the subjects so that none of them get too close to the edge of the stage during their "sleep walking." Then go to each in turn, and say sharply, "Stop! Every muscle of your body is frozen in that position. You cannot move!" The subjects stand like statues in whatever position they happened to be when you gave them the command.

Return back to the seated group of entranced subjects, rapidly walk to each, touch him or her on the hand and say, "Follow every suggestion that I give you." This serves to focus their attention strongly as you suggest, "There are two things I want

138

you to remember: when I reach the count of 'five' you will be wide awake and feeling fine, but also you will find that you cannot lower your arms no matter how hard you try even when you are awake. You will not be able to lower your arms until I snap my fingers by your ear...then, and only then, will your arms lower. Remember, when I reach the count of 'five' you will be wide awake, but you will be totally unable to lower your arms until I snap my fingers beside your ear. And secondly, remember this – the moment I point my finger directly at your forehead you will instantly go to sleep no matter what you may be doing. Remember, the moment I point my fingers at your forehead you will go instantly asleep. All ready now, get set to wake with your arms frozen out straight in front of you. One...two...three... four...FIVE!"

The subjects awaken in various stages of surprise at finding themselves unable to lower their arms. Their arms still seem "asleep," but otherwise they are fully awake. The five standing subjects also awaken with their arms cateleptic.

Carefully observe the variety of reactions to this group test as it is important. Here is your opportunity to spot the somnambulistic subjects you will wish to use in the advanced hypnotic tests shortly to come in your show.

If a subject responds forcefully to this posthypnotic suggestion, then you know he is one of those you will use. *The ability to judge your subjects well and to use them correctly in the performance of the various tests of which they are capable is the mark of an expert hypnotist.*

When this test of "the frozen arms" has proceeded long enough to prove its full effect, rapidly release each person by snapping your fingers beside his ear. Also request the standing subjects, as they are released, to return to their seats. You are now ready for the next emperiment.

THE CIGARETTE TEST. Turn and directly address the audience, "Amazing as some of these experiments seem upon stage, ladies and gentlemen, the real wonders of hypnotism come from its clinical value. For example, in the way it can be employed to correct habits such as smoking and drinking. Let me illustrate its power by removing the cigarette habit from someone.

Turn towards the committee and ask, "Who among you smokes cigarettes?"

Select from amongst your responsive subjects someone who smokes. Have him step forward and take a seat center stage. Next, conduct a little quiz, asking him how long he has smoked, how many cigarettes he smokes each day, if by way of an experiment he would be willing to overcome the habit, etc.

Finally, have him light a cigarette and ask him how it tastes? He'll say, "Fine," and smile in satisfaction. Then request him to look directly into your eyes, to think of himself as floating far, far away, floating into a deep hypnotic sleep. . .*and then, point your finger directly at his forehead.* Instantly the posthypnotic suggestion you have given goes into action, and he drops over his chair sound asleep in hypnosis.

The audience will gasp at this demonstration of instantaneous hypnosis!

Then suggest to the hypnotic, "Now we are together going to master a habit that you have had for a long time -- the habit of smoking. You will find that the next time you smoke, that you will no longer like the cigarette. It will taste dry and parched in your mouth. It will taste like soggy old straw. You won't care for cigarettes anymore, in fact you will hate cigarettes they taste so bad. They make your mouth all dry and parched. You will throw them away in disgust. And they make you choke and cough. Even the smoke makes you choke and cough, You dislike even the smell of smoke."

As you give the above suggestions commenting on disliking the smoke, *hold the smoking cigarette directly under the subject's nose,* and continue to suggest, "You hate the smell of even the cigarette smoke. You want to get away from it. Turn your head away from that smoke." Almost immediately the subject will cough and sneeze, a disgusted curl come on his lips, and he will turn his head away from the smoke. This occurrence is your cue to climax your suggestions with, "All right now, when I say 'three' you will open your eyes and you will find that you positively hate cigarettes, they make you sneeze and cough, you cannot smoke them anymore. You will throw the cigarette away in disgust. All right. One. . .two. . .THREE. Open your eyes and try the cigarette and see what you think of it now!"

You will note that you have not entirely awakened the subject in this test, but merely suggested that he open his eyes for its performance. The test would very probably work equally well posthypnotically, but for the purpose of this stage demonstration let him remain in a sort of half trance. Proceed right on:

"Here, try the cigarette." Force it between the subject's lips, and say, "Take a good puff of the cigarette. How you hate it. You hate that cigarette. Throw it away in disgust!"The subject will take a drag, cough, sputter, and throw the cigarette from him with vengeance.

You turn and address the audience, "You see here an example of how a habit can be rapidly removed through hypnosis. This subject has admitted that he has smoked cigarettes for a number of years, and yet, in less than two minutes time, he now finds himself utterly unable to smoke. Let us check this with a different brand of cigarettes. Will someone lend me a cigarette please."

Someone either from the committee or the audience obliges.

You hand the cigarette to the subject, place it to his lips, and light it for him, as you say, "You will find this one will taste ten times as bad as the other one. Oh, how you hate cigarettes."

The subject will again cough and sputter, much to the amusement of the spectators who throughly enjoy this human interest sort of thing, and will throw the cigarette far from him. Now suggest, "Let's bring the old good taste back again, shall we? Look me in the eyes. Your eyes are growing heavy already close them and go to sleep!" Your subject already in half trance will respond immediately. You carry on with the suggestions:

"In a moment, I will count from one to five. At the count of 'five' you will be wide awake and feeling fine. And you will find that cigarettes taste all good and sweet again, just as they always have. All ready now, I will count from one to five, and at the count of 'five' you will be wide awake, and will enjoy smoking just like you always have. One. . .two. . .three. . .four. . .FIVE." The subject awakens, you offer him a cigarette which he now smokes with obvious enjoyment.

An effect of this nature is important to the stature of your show; it impresses the spectators with the clinical and practical value of hypnotism.

As he has proved a good subject, there is no need to dismiss this man you have just used in the cigarette test, as he can take part in the next one also. And select out six of seven other subjects from the committee as well. *Select subjects you have previously noted as being responsive to posthypnotic suggestions.* Ask them to move their chairs forward and form a line near the center of the stage. Have everyone take a seat.

Group Hypnotizing From Audience Experiment

You are now going to introduce a sensational test in your show also it is one that closely identifies you with the spectators as you are going to hypnotize from in their midst. You address the audience:

"Ladies and gentlemen, I will now show you a type of hypnotic demonstration that is very rarely performed, the hypnotizing of a group of persons all at the same time, from the rear of the audience."

Then to the front row of expectant subjects explain, "I am going right down into the audience, and from that distance hypnotize you. So pay very close attention to me, and concentrate with all of your ability.

And to the audience again, say, "And you in the audience can assist me a great deal in this difficult experiment, if you, too, will hold in your minds the idea of these subjects, here on the stage, going down deep into the hypnotic trance."

It is this intimate interplay between stage and audience that makes the hypnotism show different from any other. It is great entertainment.

Then, just before you leave the stage, turn towards the committee, and add, "Now primarily I am going to concentrate on these subjects here in the front row, but if there are others in the back group who wish to also participate in the experiment, feel free to do so, and concentrate right along with them. All right everyone, sit back in your chairs, feet together, hands in your lap, and all ready for this experiment in hypnotism from the rear of the audience."

You have arranged your presentation psychologically so your conditions for this dramatic test are pretty well set for its success even before you start. The row of eight subjects in front represent some of the most responsive hypnotics in the group, so they are persons who are almost certain to go readily into hypnosis. Some of the remaining committee members are also good subjects, and you have paved the way for them likewise, to enter hypnosis if they choose to follow. Frequently many do as subjects come to enjoy being hypnotized. Those who do enter trance in the course of the experiment, you can then bring forward to join the front group of selected subjects. The subjects who do not respond are all seated to the back of the stage anyway, and are not bothersome. Just let them sit there as observers of the action, and their merriment at the hypnotics' reactions will only add to the general enjoyment of the audience. You are now ready to perform this feat.

Go down into the audience, walk deep into the midst of the spectators and stand on an aisle seat near the back row in the auditorium. Call out to your subjects on stage to look directly at you in the audience.

You suggest, "As you all look out here at me in the audience, and concentrate your attention towards my eyes, already even over this great distance you begin to feel the hypnotic effects of sleep coming upon you each and everyone. You are becoming sleepy and the hypnotic trance is coming over you. Your eyes are getting heavy, and the lids want to close. Close those tired eyes and sleep."

From your stance at the rear of the audience, dramatically point your right forefingers out towards the subjects on the distant stage *in a sweeping arc so it cover each of them.* That pointing forefingers conveys a posthypnotic cue to reenter hypnosis, and almost at once the subjects on stage will close their eyes, start to nod, and go to sleep. You will amaze even yourself at how rapidly the hypnotics will respond at this point in your show, and to the spectators it is positively astonishing!

You now commence your "sleep formula" to the subjects, stating, "You are all going to sleep, deep, deep asleep, etc." as you walk up the aisle back onto the stage from the rear of the audience. Stand behind the subject on the right end of the front group first. Stroke his forehead a few times, press on his shoulders so he slumps in his chair, and push his hands off his lap so that they dangle limply at his sides, as you continue to suggest, "Nothing will bother you in the slightest. You are sleeping deeply in perfect peace. Keep on going down deeper and deeper to sleep."

Then go to the subject next in line sleeping beside him, and repeat the process. Just before you pass on to the next subject in the row, push the heads of the first and second subject together so that they support each other while they sleep. This is a very whimsical bit of business See Fig. 52.

Fig. 52

Fig. 53

Front Group of Subjects Experiments
REVOLVING ARMS TEST. When all of the front row of subjects are sleeping peacefully, look at your back group, and if any others in the committee are asleep in hypnosis also, go to them and push their heads down into their laps, as you instruct them to go on sleeping down yet deeper.

Then go back to the first subject in the front row, lift up his hands, turn them parallel to each other, and start them rotating rapidly around and around each other, as you say to him, "Keep those hands revolving. They will not stop. The more you try to stop them the faster they go. Try and stop them. You cannot. They are revolving faster and faster." Work rapidly down the row until every one of the subjects is rapidly revolving their arms around each other. See Fig. 53.

Then say to the group, "Your hands are revolving around faster and faster. You cannot stop them. But when I say 'three' they will instantly stop, and freeze in that position, and you will find you cannot move them try as hard as you will. When I say 'three' your revolving hands will instantly stop and freeze dead still in the air. One ... two ... THREE!"

Instantly the revolving arms freeze still in the air. The subjects can't move them try as hard as they will. Then suggest, "When I say 'go,' around and around your hands will revolve again." Suddenly shout, "GO!" Immediately the hands commence to revolve in a frenzy, as you suggest, "Around and around they go, faster and faster and faster!"

While all the subjects' arms are revolving at a pitch, step quietly behind the first subject of the row, make a few hypnotic passes without contact in front of his face, and softly suggest directly into his ear, "It is all going away. You are going back to sleep. Your arms are dropping to your lap. You are going fast to sleep.

The visible transformation of moods that flit across the subject's face as he slips from violent motion into peaceful slumber is fascinating to behold. Push his hands off his lap so that they dangle at his sides, and leave him sleeping as you pass from one subject to the next, leaving each sleeping in turn, until the entire front row of subjects are all again sleeping soundly.

THE CANARY BIRD TEST. Then address the front group, "At the count of 'three' you will all open your eyes, and you will see perched on the fingers of your left hand the cutest little canary bird you ever saw. You will love this little bird, and will have a wonderful time playing with it.

"All ready now, get ready to play with the little bird. Sit back in your chair and hold out your left hand, so you can look at the little bird." The subjects will respond, adjusting themselves in their chairs and holding out their left hands perch-like, as you repeat the suggestions, "Remember, at the count of 'three' you will open your eyes and look directly at your left hand, and perched on it you will see the cutest, little, yellow canary bird you ever saw. And as you look at it, and play with it, it will send you down deeper and deeper into hypnosis all the time. Get ready now to look at that little yellow bird in your left hand. One ... two ... THREE!"

The subjects open their eyes, stare at their left fingers, as you continue, "Pat that little bird. Isn't it cute? Hold it gently. Let it hop onto your lap if it wants to." The subjects will begin going through a variety of pantomines of patting and playing with the little bird.

Advance to one of the subjects who is responding well, place your finger in his left palm and then waft it in the air, as you say, "There goes the little bird flying about. Catch it! Catch it!" The subject will grab air trying to catch it. Then tell him to chase it, and he will leave his seat, chasing the imaginary canary about the stage.

Make "the little bird" fly about from the hands of a few other subjects until you have plenty of action going on stage. *Be sure to keep a careful eye on the subjects as they move about the stage to make sure no one gets too close to the footlights.* Forewarned is forearmed; always safeguard your subjects.

In this regard, always keep in mind this important rule of hypnotic showmanship, the hypnotic can become so fully absorbed in the performance of your suggestions that he will fail to look out for himself, so it becomes your duty to watch out for his welfare during your show.

Then go to each subject who is trying to catch the imaginary bird, and say, "Here it is, here is the little bird," as you pretend to catch it. Hand it to him, and add, "Hold it gently but don't let it get away." The subject will at once cup his hands carefully, and you suggest, "Take it and go back to your seat."

When all of the subjects are again in their seats, patting "the bird," step behind the subject seated at the end of the row, make a few passes in front of his face and suggest, "You are getting sleepy again. The little bird is all gone now. Forget all about the little bird and go sound, sound to sleep." As the subject slumps over in trance, whisper directly into his ear so that only he can hear the posthypnotic suggestion here repeated, "Remember, the moment I point my finger at your forehead you will go instantly asleep."

Going to each of the subjects in turn you place them again in trance, quietly repeating to each the posthypnotic suggestion, *"Remember, the moment I point my finger at your forehead you will go instantly asleep."* In this subtle handling, you have prepared your subjects for the test in instaneous hypnotism which is to follow.

To conclude "The Canary Bird Test," save the subject who is showing the most reaction to the "canary" for the last, and when all the others are sleeping peacefully with the exception of him, walk over by his side and say, "Let me show you a magic trick. I call it the vanishing canary bird trick. Hold the little bird perched right on your fingers directly before your eyes. That's it. Fine. Now watch very closely, for I am going to count very slowly from one to three, and at the count of 'three' that canary will disappear right before your eyes, and you won't know where it goes, and you will look all around trying to find the vanished canary. Here we go, watch closely! One ... two ... three ... the bird is GONE!"

The subject will stare in stark amazement as the bird disappears right before his eyes, and will begin searching all about the stage trying to discover where it went, to the delight of the audience.

After the fun has proceeded long enough, quickly return the subject to a deep sleep among the committee.

INSTANTANEOUS HYPNOTISM TEST. Turn and speak directly to the audience, "Ladies and gentlemen, you are about to witness what has been called the fastest demonstration of hypnotism on the stage today. *Instantaneous Hypnosis.* It is something you will remember as long as you live."

Go to one of the subjects in the row. Have him stand up and move about. Ask him if he is sure that he is wide awake and feels perfectly normal. When he assures you that he does, have him move his chair a little forward from the group and take his seat. *Then,* suddenly point your finger directly at him, and exclaim, "SLEEP!" Instantly the subjects drops over in a trance.

It is a very impressive demonstration.

Then suggest to the subject, "When you wake up again at the count of 'five' you will feel perfectly normal in all ways, but you will find that you are stuck to the seat of your chair. You cannot get out of that chair pull as hard as you will for you are glued tight to the seat. You cannot get out of your seat, until I clap my hands, then you will come instantly free! All ready, at the count of 'five' you will again be wide awake. One...two...three...four...FIVE."

The subject awakens, you ask him to try and rise from his chair; but he is stuck tight. He tugs and struggles but cannot get free. Right while he is in the middle of a violent tug, suddenly clap your hands, and he will leap from his seat! Thank the subject, and have him return his chair to the row and be seated.

Then quietly walk past the row of subjects, turn suddenly on a subject, catch his eye, point your finger directly at his forehead, and say, "SLEEP!" Instantly he is hypnotized. Then hypnotize two other subjects in the same manner. The way the hypnotics, one moment wide awake, and then suddenly with a little gasp slump over instantly into hypnosis is uncanny. The test builds amazement upon amazement and is something the spectators will never forget. It looks like a miracle.

THE AMNESIA TEST. Three subjects are now deeply entranced, as you address the audience, "You have all heard tales of missing persons who show up strangely in different cities, and yet when questioned by the police seem utterly unable to remember their names, where they are from, or anything about themselves. Such persons are called amnesia victims, amnesia being a peculiar mental condition characterized by lose of

146

memory.

"Now, this state of amnesia can be experimentally demonstrated through hypnosis. Let us attempt such an experiment." Turn towards your three sleeping subjects and say, "In a moment, I am going to awaken you, and when you wake up a strange thing will have happened. You will feel fine in every way and be perfectly normal, except that you will find you cannot remember your name when you try to do so. Also you will not have the slightest idea of where you are, how you got here, and anything about themselves. Your minds will be a complete blank. You won't remember your own names, where you are, or anything about yourselves...until I snap my fingers beside your ear, then everything will come back to you instantly. Remember now, after you awaken you will feel fine in every way, but you will not be able to recall your own names, who you are, or anything about yourselves ... until I snap my fingers beside your ear, then everything will come back to you in a flash. Ready now. At the count of 'five' you will be wide awake and feeling fine. One ...two ... three ... four ...FIVE."

The subjects awaken with a sort of blank look on their faces. You bring one of them forward to the front of the stage and ask a few questions, just as a police sergeant would do, as, "How do you feel?" The subject answers, "Fine." "Would you like to tell the audience your name?" The subject looks blank and appears uncomfortable. "Well, what is your name? No response. Well, if you can't remember who you are, then tell us where you are?" The subject thinks hard and shakes his head in bewilderment. "Alright now, keep thinking hard and see what happens." You suddenly snap your fingers beside his ear. Immediately the blank look vanishes from his face, and the subject smiles relieved as you again ask, "Can you tell us your name now?" The subject answers,"Of course," and states his name. You thank him and he resumes his seat.

Call the second subject forward, let us say you use a girl this time for variety, and you repeat the test. She is totally unable to give her name or tell anything about herself until you snap your fingers by her ear.

It is extremely interesting to observe the many variety of responses the subjects will go through as they react to such an experience. Some will tend to get panicky while others will take it all with stoic calmness. When the test is complete, thank the young lady, gesture her to her seat, and explain to the audience:

"You have seen here, ladies and gentlemen, some examples of experimentally produced amnesia. In normal life, the amnesia is usually produced through a mental conflict within the individual from which the person tries to hide by retreating into this condition. Basically, from a psychological standpoint, there is very little difference between spontaneously produced amnesia and that induced through hypnotism. Let us test this last subject."

You bring the subject forward and proceed with the test by asking him various questions about himself that he seems utterly unable to answer. His amnesia is complete. You ask him what he intends to do about it to get out of his predicament? Some subjects get quite concerned about the matter. Then, to climax the experiment you borrow a small hand mirror and hold it up directly in front of the subject's face, as you ask:

"Whom do you see in the mirror?" The subject usually will say, "A face." "Is it a nice face?" you ask. "Do you like it?" The subject shakes his head. "All right now, watch that face close in the mirror and see what happens. Suddenly snap your fingers; the subject starts, smiles, and sheepishly admits that it is his face he sees in the mirror.

Modern audiences very much appreciate a scientific test of this nature. It gives credence to the hypnotism show.

Seventh Group Experiment:

The Motion Picture Test On Committee

You are now going to perform one of the most entertaining of all stage hypnotism demonstrations. A test that literally convulses the audience.

Stand in front of your row of subjects, ask them to look at you, and hypnotize the entire group very quickly with a few suggestions of sleep while making use of the posthypnotic cue of pointing your finger directly towards them, as you sweep it slowly from one end of the line to the other. When the members of the committee are all in deep hypnosis, go rapidly to each and push them farther down in their chair, as you repeat to each individual quickly, "Sleep, sleep deep." Then address the committee as a body:

"In a moment, you will all open your eyes and you will see before you a motion picture screen, and on it is playing a very exciting western movie. You are going to have a wonderful time watching this picture. You will see the hero and heorine. You will see the villian and the comic, and you will have the time of your life watching this motion picture unreel before your eyes.

"Get ready, everybody, to watch this motion picture. Sit up straight in your chair, and at the count of 'three' open your eyes and watch the movie. All ready, one ...two ...THREE! Open your eyes and watch the movie."

The subjects all open their eyes, and staring out excitedly if front of themselves lean forward in their chairs, as you suggest, "Now the picture is getting very exciting. You're having a wonderful time. You are getting so excited watching that picture.

And here comes the comedian. Say, isn't he the funny fellow! You never saw anyone so funny, you just want to laugh and laugh and laugh. Go ahead, laugh and laugh."

Give your suggestions in this test with the enthusiam of a sport's announcer, and as you narrate the happenings in the imaginary motion picture interpret it in your voice. Your interpretation of mood functions as much in the way of suggestions to which hypnotics respond as do your words. When you say, for example, "laugh," *really laugh.* And how the subjects will respond. They will be literally convulsed with laughter. Laughter is contagious, and the audience will be laughing right along with the subjects.

And right when the laughter is at its peak, suddenly change the mood, and suggest, "Say, the picture is not funny anymore, the movie is getting sad. Look there is a poor little old lady out in the snow freezing to death, and her tiny grandchildren are in the log cabin starving to death. Oh, it is so sad. You feel so sad. You've never felt more sad at any movie. It makes you want to cry."

The quick transformation of moods is astonishing as the subjects immediately shift from gales of laughter to saddness, and begin to cry.

Then suddenly suggest, "Look everything is alright now, the old lady is back in her warm cabin and there is plenty of food on the table to feed the children. And, look, the motion picture is getting funny again. You want to laugh at it. Laugh" Go ahead and laugh and laugh!"

Get all of the subjects laughing once more, then step behind each in turn, pass your hand slowly in front of each person's face and the hypnotic goes to sleep. It's laughter to sleep. It's amazing. You simply suggest to each subject, "The motion picture is fading away now. It is all gone. You are going down sound to sleep." And down they go, one by one, until all are sleeping soundly, and you are ready to perform your concluding test.

The Posthypnotic Climax To the Hypnotism Show

Turn and address the audience, "Ladies and gentlemen, to conclude the program I will show you now a demonstration in mass posthypnotic suggestion. I believe you will find it highly thought-provoking. As you witness these demonstrations in hypnotism unquestionly you will find many of them amusing, for entertainment is our purpose. But look beyond the humor and appreciate the remarkable qualities of mental control these show. These volunteers have learned, in this short time, how to control their subconscious mind. They can use the ability to take away pain in having a tooth filled at the dentist. They can use it to overcome unwanted habits. They can use it to increase their memory, develop self-confidence, and use the power invested in hypnosis in many useful ways for better living. It is a wonderful mental skill.

"And now I am going to awaken the entire group. And when they wake up everyone will feel just wonderful and fine, and good all over. Notice how pleasant, gradual, and gentle the awakening from hypnosis is, and everyone will awaken just feeling fine. And watch, also, mass posthypnosis.

Turn and address your sleeping hypnotics, "You have all had a wonderful time at the show, and you can use the hypnotic skill you have learned in many ways to help yourselves. It can bring you confidence and success. And you have had a wonderful sleep and relaxing experience. When you wake up in just a moment, you will feel refreshed and fine. BUT here a strange thing, when you awaken and try to leave the stage, you will discover that your left foot is stuck to the floor. And pull and tug as hard as you can, you will not be able to free your left foot ... until I snap my fingers by your ear ... then your left foot will come free, but your right foot will then get stuck to the stage.

"All right, I will now count slowly from one to five. With every count you will gradually wake up, and by the time I reach 'five' be wide, wide awake. BUT you will find you cannot leave the stage because your left foot will be glued, stuck to the floor... and it will not come free, but your right foot will then become stuck.. until I snap my fingers again when your right foot will come free but your left foot will get stuck to the floor all over again. And so it will go back and forth...first one foot stuck to the floor and then the other everytime I snap my fingers, until I clap my hands loudly beside you, and say it is all gone.

"All ready now. I will count from one to five, and by the time I reach 'five' you will all be wide awake and feeling fine, BUT you cannot leave this stage because your left foot is glued and stuck to the floor. Ready, one ... two ... three .. four ... and FIVE. Everyone wide awake and feeling fine!"

Addressing the now awake committee members, you say, "Allow me, at this time, to thank each and everyone of you for your splendid cooperation and fine powers of concentration, and now if you will try to return to your seats, please."

The subjects start to leave the stage and pandemonium ensues, as everyone finds to his or her amazement that their left foot is stuck to the floor. Confusion reigns supreme as they pull and tug trying to free their foot. You pass to each and snap your fingers by their ear; their left foot comes free, but the right is now stuck fast to the stage. More finger snapping, and first one foot and then the other gets stuck. Finally, you slap your hands loudly beside one subject as you say, "All right, it's all gone. You are free to leave the stage," and he gingerly picks up his feet, looks at his soles, and marches off the stage.

As the subject leaves encourage the audience to give him a nice round of applause. Do this for each subject as he or she is dismissed from the stage so each person may receive recognition for their hypnotic performance during the show.

Free another subject, and then another. They march off the stage and return to their seats in the audience. The next person you release you walk over with to the side of the stage as though to escort him to the steps, and just when you get to the side pillar you suddenly place his hand flat against the wall, and say, "Your hand is stuck there, you cannot pull it free." Heightened suggestibility remains with the subject for a time after coming out of hypnosis, he will still be in a responsive mood, and his hand will instantly become stuck to the post. Leave him there tugging, and release another subject or so.

Then walk to the front of the stage, and just as one of your subjects is in the aisle to return to his seat, ask him to turn about and look at you, and as he does so hold out your right forefinger and say, "Your eyes are fixed to the tip of my fingers. See, you sway about as it sways. Your eyes are closing. You are sinking, sinking, your knees are sagging. Knees sagging. Dropping right down to the floor in the aisle." The subject still in a hypnotic mood, will instantly respond; he begins to sway and sags down to the floor. It is an impressive demonstration of hypnotism.

This test performed right in their midst, as it were, is very dramatic and brings the power of hypnotism forcefully home to every spectator. End the test by quickly clapping your hands, and say, "All right, the influence is all gone now. You are wide awake, and you feel just fine."

Then dash quickly about the stage, release the subject stuck to the side post and all the rest of the subjects except one, whom you apparently overlooked in your feverish activities of freeing all of the subjects. Thus the stage is clear with the exception of this last subject still valiantly tugging at his stuck foot. You continue to apparently absent-mindedly over look him as you advance to the front of the stage to give your closing remarks to the audience.

"And so, ladies and gentlemen, you have witnessed a gamut of demonstration of some of the interesting and unusual aspects of the science of hypnotism. On behalf of the volunteers and myself, let me thank you for your most courteous attention, and bid you a pleasant good evening."

All during these salutatory remarks, various members of the audience will be calling up trying to remind you that you have overlooked one subject who is still stuck on stage. You appear oblivious to this. Suddenly you seem to catch on, turn and spot the subject, and with a tongue-in-cheek apology, dash to him, clap your hands and release him. Walk with this last subject to the side of the stage, shake him by the hand, thank him for volunteering, and let him return to his seat. Take your final bow ending the show, and exit.

This entire last sequence should be performed with as much dash and verve as you can manage to put into it. Heap action upon action. Lift your audience up to a fever pitch of laughter and excitement, and then the last humorous bit of seemingly overlooking the remaining subject provides a marvelous concluding tag. In showbusiness, *its a topper!*

Of such is the designing of the hypnotism show.

17

Further Experiments
in Stage Hypnotism

The hypnotism show described in the last chapter is one I have performed internationally. It is not expected that you will have occasion to use it in toto, for obviously the show of one performer will not necessarily be suitable for another. However, it will serve to illustrate details of presentation and handling, methods of routining, and the variety of effects possible which will serve to assist you in creating your own show.

Being creative is the secret of art. In this chapter, You will find an additional variety of hypnotic effects. All of these I have used at various times. Some of them may possibly prove useful in aiding you in creating demonstrations that best suit you personally in designing your own entertainment with hypnotism. Further, in chapter eighteen will be found a collection of the routines of many world famous hypnotists, some of which unquestionably you can adapt to your own show. You have ample material to work with to develop a wonder-filled hypnotic program that is entirely your own production.

As you now know the method, and have studied in detail the pattern in the successful giving of suggestions to produce the various hypnotic situations, I will henceforth present only the outline and general theme of each experiment. The exact wording of the suggestions you can supply as necessary from your own practice and experience. You will thus become a creative artist.

Drawing a Subject Across the Stages
This is an experiment in waking suggestion and fits in well with your "Falling Backwards and Forwards Tests."

Stand the subject at one side of the stage while you stand on the opposite side. Face the subject and stretch your hands out towards him, commence making pulling passes in toward yourself while suggesting that he is coming forwards towards you, that he will not fall, but will take a step forward, and, step by step, will be drawn clear across the stage to you.

The Linked Hands Test On the Committee
Another experiment in waking suggestion that ties in excellently with "The Locked Hands Test" is this one in which all the subjects join hands together. You suggest that their hands are becoming locked to each other, and that they cannot release their grips try as hard as they will. The resulting struggle of the entire group to release their hands is spectacular.

Subject Going to Sleep in the Audience

This test is another of the type which promotes the unique performer audience relationship which is possible in the hypnotism show. While a subject is sleeping in hypnosis on the stage, give him a posthypnotic suggestion that when he awakens he will return to his seat in the audience, and the moment he takes his seat he will go to sleep right in the midst of the spectators.

The effect is sensational. Dash from the stage down to the sleeping subject and awaken him.

An Age Regression Experiment For Use on the Stage

Tell the hypnotic that he is going to imagine himself going back through the years, that he is but two years old, and is attending a birthday party. The subject will act and respond as a two-year old. This test can be made a feature of your show. Serious age regression experiments do not belong in the realm of stage hypnotisn, but a purely imaginary age regression of this type in fun form is safe and very effective.

The Age Advancement Experiment

Tell a hypnotized subject that he is going ahead in time, is advancing upwards through the years, that he is ninety years of age, and is stiff and aged. The resulting pantomine is astonishing. Here is another feature for your show. This test can be combined with the foregoing as they form a logical sequence in dramatic action when performed with the same hypnotic.

Dramatized Personality Changing On the Stage

Suggest to your hypnotic that he is some character very different from his normal personality; such as a newsboy, sailor, politician, etc. The resulting characterizations would do justice to a polished actor.

Theme Hypnosis: A Trip to Mars

Here's a test with a science fiction theme. Tell the subjects to watch and that they will see a flying saucer coming in for a landing. Tell them to scramble aside as it makes a landing. Then tell them that they are now inside the flying saucer, and are traveling through space. Finally they land on Mars and go outside to walk around in their space suits on the surface of the planet. Suggest that the gravity is slight, so they walk around like they are walking on a rubber mattress. Then bring them back to earth. Its a sensational test and very contemporary.

Singing and Playing an Instrument While in Hypnosis

Tell the hypnotic to sing or play a musical instrument, and he will oblige most willingly. Unless he possesses actual talent a concert is hardly to be expected, but his earnestness in playing is most interesting to watch. The subject will even play upon an imaginary instrument, if you wish to design the test that way.

Changing the Sex of a Hypnotized Person

Tell a male subject that he is a woman, and then place him in a female situation such as frantically trying to escape from a mouse. Conversely, tell a hypnotized female subject that she is a man, and is delivering a speech at the local Rotary Club luncheon about civic improvements. Tests of this nature make fine stage demonstrations.

The Wonderful Penny Hypnotic Tests

Place a penny in each of your hypnotized subjects' palms, and suggest that it is getting very heavy, so heavy that they cannot lift it out of their palm as it is too heavy. The subjects will all try to pick the penny up but cannot do so. Then say the penny's weight has become normal again, but that it is getting hot and that they had better get rid of it before it burns their hand. The way the subjects flip those pennies away is a riot.

The "Hot Seat" Hypnotic Test

A similar test to the latter part of the above, is to suggest to your group of hypnotics that the seats of their chairs are getting hot, and while such will not harm them in anyway, they had better get out of those chairs pronto. Up they go in a surge!

The Imaginary "Airplane Trip" Group Hypnotic Test

This is a group hallucination test with the entire committee. Tell them that they are all going on an airplane trip, and are most enthusiastic about it. Then describe the trip, step by step, viz.: leaving the ground, looking over the side of the plane, sighting objects on the ground below, and finally landing. The individual responses of the different subjects as they react to the various suggested situations according to their individual natures makes this a spectacular test.

The Great Hypnotic Marching Band Feat

I featured this test while playing the Kerridge Odeon Theatres in New Zealand. Tell the hypnotics to line up on stage ready for marching. Each subject is to play their favorite band instrument (imaginary instruments) while marching; one has a bass drum, sousaphone, french horn, trombone, etc. Leading the group (use your most animated subject for this part) is the drum major. Explain to subjects that when the march music starts they will march from the stage, down the asiles, going around the auditorium playing their instruments, and will then march back onto the stage. Each person will then return to their seat and go back to sleep. When the marching music begins the march starts, and around they go. Its a wonderful test, and presents that excellent stage/audience relationship which is possible in the hypnotism show.

Group Temperature Changing: The Hot and Cold Test

Here is another feature for the hypnotism show. Suggest to the hypnotized committee members that they are in the middle of a desert and it is becoming very hot, the sun is blazing down upon them, and it is so hot they just can't sit still any longer. Tell them that they just must try to get cool, to open their collars, take off their coats, etc. The stage action is very exciting.

When the subjects have all become obviously very hot, change your suggestion to just the opposite extreme, and say, "Now the heat is all going away and you are becoming very cold, you are shivering. Put your coats back on and bundle up." This instant shifting in temperature is very impressive to an audience. End the experiment by suggesting that everyone is at normal temperature again and feels perfectly comfortable.

A Word to the Wise Regarding Stage Hypnotic Experiments

Always show good taste in every hypnotic demonstration you present. Good humor and laughter is always enjoyed by everyone, but be sure that the laughter is never produced at the expense of the subjects, it must be the genuine kind that results from a funny situation.

As a hypnotic showman, never present any tests which poke ridicule at your subjects; *make it your rule never to use experiments that in anyway would make your subjects regret that they volunteered to come onto the stage. Further, avoid all tests that are dangerous or could cause harm to the subjects. Keep all your experiments on a harmless fun level and it will be enjoyed by everyone, while still providing astounding entertainment.*

The aim of the modern professional stage hypnotist is to make his entire show a pleasureable experience for both subjects and spectators.

18
A Potpourri of
Hypnotic Routines

If this book contained nothing other than the material in this chapter I would consider it of superlative value. Here are the basic patterns of the routines of famous stage hypnotists from many parts of the world. I look upon routines as the very *entertainment* heart of professional stage hypnotism, for it is not so much how well you hypnotize as it is what you do with your hypnotized subjects that makes the show. Clever routines illustrate through suggestion a distortion of expected human behavior that is at once ludicrous and amazing. *Such is why hypnotism is entertaining.*

Actually, all I can do is sketch the skeletons of the routines for you, what is done with them to produce entertainment depends entirely upon the individual skill of the performer. In all forms of show presentations, routines must be mastered throughly so as to present such as a work-of-art. This applies to all entertainers, singers, dancers, magicians, comedians, hypnotists, whatever the talent being presented. It is *how* the routines are presented that lifts the show from mediocre to "big time." Intense work and long practice must go into complete mastering of a routine to make it perform well and flow along as smooth entertainment.

In presenting hypnotic routines, always be definite in giving instruction to the subjects so they will know precisely what is expected of them, and what they are to do. Some subjects are highly creative and spontaneous, and only the bare suggestion of the routine idea is sufficient. However, other subjects will be found to be unimaginative and lethargic. As a practical showman, don't leave too much to your subjects' imaginations by being too general in your suggestions. *Be specific!* Plan your suggestions carefully to describe exactly the reactions you want to have occur. Handled so, your routines will run along fluidly, and you will obtain the effects you have planned in your programming.

I will now outline a large assortment of professional hypnotic routines. All of these routines will be found to present amusing and/or dramatic situations with mass audience entertainment appeal. They may be modified and developed as the individual performer wishes. Some of the routines can be effectively handled with one subject, worked on several at the same time, or performed on the entire group all at once. It will be found that some tests are most effective when attention is concentrated upon one or so subjects, while others work best with the entire committee participating. Likewise, some routines will be found most effective when worked while the subject(s) are in hypnosis, (entranced), while others are most dramatic as posthypnotic effects. *Experience under fire in the actual performing situation before audiences will determine your best presentation.*

As you have learned, in presenting each routine to the subject(s) always include in your suggestions a definite "cue" to terminate each operation in which the hypnotic may be engaged, such as suggesting,"When I clap my hands the effects are you are experiencing will instantly cease." Planting such a termination cue will make it possible for you to end each test in a clean manner at the climax of its audience impact, as well as clear the suggestion from each subject in a precise and clean-cut manner.

Program your show together in the most effective sequences possible. My personal hypnotism show, as previously gone through in detail, will serve an example of this handling. Remember, the hypnotism show must be good theatre. You have a fine selection of material to work with. *Plan your show carefully featuring the effects that work best for you and provide the best entertainment for the audience.*

Whatever routines you choose to perform, learn each throughly so you can present such as second nature. Master every suggestion, every gesture, every bit of staging. Rehearse your entire show so that it flows along as one continuous unit smooth entertainment. *Precision in presentation is the mark of the polished performer. And, let's reemphasize, its not what you do that is especially important, its how you do what you do.*

A COLLECTION OF SEVENTY-FIVE SUCCESSFUL HYPNOTIC ROUTINES

(These routines have taken years to develop . . .indeed it has taken years just to collect them. They represent *treasure* to the stage hypnotist.)

1. Tell the subject that when he wakes up he will light a cigarette, that when you snap your fingers he will be unable to draw on it, but will blow out through it instead.
2. Tell the subject that he will be unable to drink from a glass of water no matter how hard he tries; that he will spill the water all over in the attempt to drink it.
3. Tell the subject that he cannot light a cigarette no matter how hard he tries.
4. Tell the subject that he cannot place a cigarette in his mouth no matter how hard he tries until you snap your finger by his ear.
5. Give the subject a doll and a handkerchief, and tell him he is the father and that the baby needs a change of diapers; that he will try to put the diaper on but cannot fasten the pin.
6 Place a subject's thumb to his nose and tell him he cannot remove it no matter how hard he tries.

The "feeling tone" of this stunt is a bit brash, and such a test should only be presented in the proper situation. Show good taste.

7.   Similar to the above test, tell a subject to place a thumb in each ear and that he cannot pull them away no matter how hard he tries.

8.   As a posthypnotic experiment, tell a woman subject that she is displeased with her husband wearing loud neckties, and that, when she awakens, she will turn to the man nearest her, whom she will think is her husband, and will give him a lecture about his ties, but that when you snap your fingers she will be unable to utter another word until you say she can speak.

9.   Tell a subject that her shoes hurt and that she has them on backwards; that she must put the left shoe on her right foot and the right shoe on her left foot to make them comfortable. Awaken her. Its a riot when she tries to walk and notices that her shoes are on opposite feet.

10.   Tell a woman subject (who has a purse on the stage beside her) that when she awakens she will not be able to see her purse, and will look all around trying to find it.

11.   Tell a subject that there are robbers in the audience and that he has a bundle of $100.00 bills which you give him (hand him some blank paper slips), and tell him he had better hide the money in his shoes. Then awaken him, and ask him what he has in his shoes.

12.   Tell a subject that he will smoke a cigarette but that when you snap your fingers it will suddenly taste like burning rubber. This is very funny, especially when working with a group of subjects. Be sure to use only subjects who are cigarette smokers.

13.   Tell a subject that when you snap your fingers his chair will suddenly develop rubber legs, and he will bounce up and down on it.

14.   Hand the subject a glass of water and have him take a drink. Then suggest that when you snap your fingers it will suddenly taste like vinegar, and he will spit it out.

15.   Have two subjects (boy and girl) sit facing each other, and tell them they are going to hypnotize one another. The performer stands in the center back of them and gives the suggestions. As each gaze into the other's eyes they fall asleep.

16.   This test can be used in combination with the above. Suggest to girl subject that when you awaken her she will notice a chair which she will try to pick up, but that it is so heavy she cannot lift it. Awaken the subject (posthypnotic), and she tries to lift the chair but cannot do so.

Now suggest to the boy subject that when you awaken him he will see the girl trying very hard to move a chair, and that he will go to her aid to help her lift the chair, but that it is so heavy he cannot lift it either.

The fun developed from this situation is obvious. When the subjects find that they cannot lift the chair, you walk over and lift it easily. Tell the subjects to retain their hold on the chair firmly, and you let go; it immediately drops back to the stage pulling them down with it.

17.   Hand a subject a sheet of paper and tell him that he cannot tear it no matter how hard he tries.

18.   Tell a subject to grip a pencil; tell him it has become sticky with glue and that he cannot throw it away from his hands no matter how hard he tries.

19.   Tell a subject that he is stuck to the seat of his chair and that he cannot get up from it no matter how hard he tries.

20.   Tell a subject that when he awakens (posthypnotic) he will find his shoelace untied (pull shoelace loose), and that he will be unable to retie it no matter how hard he tries.

21.   Get your subjects in a row on the stage and tell them to start clapping their hands. Then tell them that they can't stop clapping, and the harder they try to stop the louder and harder they will clap. There is something about hand clapping that is very rousing to an audience.

22.   Place two subjects side-by-side and place an open book between them. Then suggest to the subject on the left that what he reads in the book will be very sad and will make him cry. Then suggest to the subject on the right that what he reads in the book is very funny and will make him laugh. Also suggest to the subjects that they will be very puzzled by the entirely opposite reactions that each gets from reading the same book. The hilarious situation resulting can be imagined.

There is a valuable point illustrated here in the development of hypnotic routines, which is to combine a variety of reactions together, as in the present instance of one subject crying from what they read, the other laughing, and the puzzlement of both over the different reaction that each has. A man and woman subject can effectively be used in tests of this nature.

23.   Male subject is told that he is a famous female movie star and is making up for an appearance at a premier. Give the subject a mirror, lipstick, eyeshadow, power and puff. The fun of seeing a man make up his face with woman's cosmetics is terrific. After the laughs have gone on long enough, and while the subject is still looking at himself in the mirror, awaken him. His surprised reaction is a riot. To end the test, give the subject a towel so he can wipe the makeup off, assure him it is all in good natured fun, and have the audience give him a big hand.

24.   Hypnotized subjects are each told that they are famous personalities. Identify each subject with a specific personality (give name of each such person, for example movie and television

stars, political figures, popular personalities in the current news). Tell them that when they awaken they will be the person named, and that the audience will applaud them when they are introduced. They are to acknowledge the applause. Awaken (posthypnotic) each subject, and introduce them to the audience by the name of the famous person you have identified each with while hypnotized. The impersonations are often amazing; this coupled with the audience applause and response to each subject makes this an outstanding test.

25.   Move star hypnotic tests are always entertaining. Here is an effective handling. Tell a male subject that one of the women subjects on the stage is a famous film star, and that he will shyly go over and ask her for a dance. The humor of the situation is obvious.

26.   Hand the subject a pair of eyeglasses (without lenses) and suggest that they are "comedy glasses." When subject looks through the glasses, everything that he sees will seem funny, and he will laugh and laugh and laugh. Its a fun test.

27.   You can combine the above "Eye Glasses Test" with the "Movie Star Test." Tell subject that when he looks through the glasses he will see various movie stars in the audience. Name a few of popular current stars. Have him look carefully through the crowd (the audience) to spot the stars. Be modern, keep up-to-date, and you will always be a popular entertainer.

28.   Tell the group of subjects that they will laugh at each other.

29.   Give a subject a pillow and tell him it is a crying baby. Say that since he is the father of the baby he must try to make it stop crying.

30.   Tell a subject that he cannot button his coat.

31.   Toss a $20.00 bill on the floor and tell the subject that he can have it if he can pick it up, but that he cannot do so as every time he reaches for the money his hand will take a wide curve away from the bill. Its sensational!

32.   Tell a group of subjects that they are walking in deep snow.

33.   Tell a group of subjects that they will open their eyes and watch a tennis match.

34.   Tell each subject that he is a musician and will play a certain instrument. Each subject is instructed that on "cue" he will play his instrument (in this test handling all instruments are entirely imaginary, each subject being told to perform on a different type of instrument). One subject is given a baton and is told that he is the conductor of the orchestra. A starting signal is given, and the "musicians" commence to play their imaginary instruments with the conductor leading them out in front.

35.   Give a woman subject a doll, and tell her it is a baby and

that she will rock and sing it to sleep.

36.   Give a subject half of a lemon, and tell him it is an apple. He will eat it with complete enjoyment.

37.   The above test can be elaborated upon and made a feature of the hypnotism show. In such regard, hypnotize a woman subject and ask her if she likes fresh peaches, plums, and oranges, and which ones she prefers. If she wishes a peach, say to her, "I am going to give you half of a nice fresh peach, and I want you to eat and enjoy it."

Hand her half of a lemon and tell her to eat it while you suggest, "My, how you do enjoy eating the nice sweet peach."

After she has eaten about half of the lemon say to her, "Now you've had enough of the peach, I am going to give you half of an orange, and I want you to take a bite out of it."

Give the subject half of an orange and let her take a bite, then suddenly suggest, "Oh, I made a mistake, I gave you half of a lemon instead of an orange." Her reaction is immediate.

Now say to her, "I was only fooling. That is really an orange, a nice sweet orange that you are eating. Taste it again, and you will see that I am right." The subject responds with satisfaction.

For a climax to the experiment, hand the subject a piece of raw potato and say, "I am going to give you a nice, juicy apple, and I want you to eat and enjoy it. While still eating with relish the potato, awaken the subject and her expression at finding herself munching on a raw piece or potato is a masterpiece of humor.

38.   Tell a man subject that he is a famous opera star and to sing a song for the audience. You can vary this by having him become a pop singer.

39.   Tell a subject that he is happy and to laugh. Now sad and to cry. If you have a very animated subject, you can suggest that he will laugh on one side of his face and cry out of the other.

40.   The Athletes Test. Tell the group of subjects that they are all athletes and are taking a series of warm up exercises. Subjects rise and sit up from their chairs. Perform pushups, etc. One subject is then brought forward and told he is a boxer practicing on his punching bag. Another is exercising on his rowing machine. With a little imagination you can develop this into one of the feature group tests of your show.

41.   Having hypnotized a group of subjects on the stage, tell them that you will awaken them now, and that you will leave the room and will hypnotize them from a distance by "telepathy." Awaken the subjects and exit from the room, leaving them seated on the stage awaiting the mental influence. As the audiences watches in awe, gradually the subjects fall asleep. You then return and wake them up. This response is actually caused by posthypnotic suggestion, but you have given another causation

for the occurrence in seeming to produce the experiment by telepathy from a distance. It is an amazing effect when presented with showmanship.

42.   Tell the subject there is a window in the center of the stage, that it is stuffy in the room, and that he will go to the window and open it to let in the fresh air. It is very funny to watch the subject open the imaginary window, especially if you unexpectedly suggest that it is stuck, and he is having difficulty getting it opened. The pantomine subjects perform while hypnotized can be astounding. Do not expect all subjects to be master pantominists however, as such skills differ with each individual. Use subjects who have proved themselves animated for such tests.

43.   Tell a girl subject that her boy friend will have disappeared when she awakens; that she will look all around trying to find him, and that after the passing of a couple of minutes he will suddenly appear seated beside her.

44.   Tell a group of girl subjects that they are in Hawaii, and that they are learning the Hula. When the music starts they will dance. Start the music and watch the fun. It is even more fun if you perform this with a group of men.

45.   Hand a subject a broom and tell him it is a beautiful girl; to sweep her up in his arms and dance with her. When the dance is over, tell him to return the girl (broom) to her seat, and wave goodbye to her.

46.   Hand some subjects each a paper plate, and tell them that they are seated in their car and are holding firmly on the wheel as they speed along. Tell them to be very careful, steer the car with great skill, and watch out for pedestrains in the crosswalks and speeders on the highway.

47.   Tell the subjects you are going to give a treat and present each with an ice cream cone. Hand an empty cone to each subject, and tell them to start licking the ice cream.

48.   Many variations on the "eating theme" are possible; subjects can go out into the country and have a picnic eating imaginary sandwiches, drinking soda pop, etc. For a climax, suggest that ants are getting into the food, and to brush them away quickly.

49.   Give a subject a broomstick and tell him it is a fishing rod, and that he is casting in his favorite stream. You can end the test by suggesting that the fishing rod is getting so heavy that he cannot hold it in his hands. He will drop it on the stage, then suggest that it is so heavy he cannot pick it up.

50.   Hand a woman subject a bottle of perfume and tell her how much she enjoys it. Suddenly suggest that you made a mistake, that it is a bottle of ammonia. Her reactions are unmistakable.

51. Tell the group of hypnotics that they will yawn, yawn, yawn, and be unable to stop yawning. The suggestions is not only effective on the subjects but on the audience as well, many of whom will yawn in unison.

52. Tell a group of subjects that there are mice running about on the floor. The reactions of the girls and even some of the men is most amusing.

53. Tell a group of subjects that they are dancing at a crowded discoteque.

54. Hand a subject a piece of rope and tell him that he cannot tie a knot in it no matter how hard he tries.

55. As a posthypnotic, tell your subject that after one minute has passed he will find his right shoe is getting very hot, so hot that he not be able to keep the shoe on; he will take it off, and that immediately he gets his right shoe off that his left shoe will then become hot and will also have to be removed. You can develop even more fun if you suggest, at the same time, that the subject will try not to attract attention to himself unduly while he takes off his hot shoes.

56. Tell a group of subjects that when they open their eyes they will see the stage covered with $100.00 bills; to scoop them up and fill their pockets with the money. Its great entertainment!

57. Tell a group of subjects to go into a garden and pick the flowers. Then to gather up the flowers into a bouquet and smell their fragrance. Now tell the girls to take the flowers and go down amongst the audience and give a flower to each baldheaded man they see, and that each time they pass out a flower to give the man a kiss on his baldhead.

58. As a posthypnotic, tell a woman subject that her name is John Smith and tell a man that his name is Mary Brown. Awaken the subjects, and ask them to introduce themselves by name to each other.

59. Tell a man subject (who is actually sitting on the stage next to a woman) that his neighbor is a man and that when he wakes up he will ask the party for a cigar. This is very funny.

60. Tell a woman subject that she is a little girl in school, and that she is to recite her favorite little poem to the students.

61. Give a subject a hat and tell him it is a dog. That he is to pet and feed it.

62. Give the subject a length of rope while you explain that it is a lasso, and get him to lasso an imaginary horse.

63. Tell a woman subject (seated at the side of the stage) that every five minutes she will come up to you and tell you that your face is dirty; she will take her handkerchief and try to wipe it for you.

64. Give a subject a wax candle and tell him it is a delicious stick of candy. The subject licks it with enjoyment. This test can

be varied by suggesting that the candle is a cigar that the subject will smoke. His expression on finding a candle in his mouth, on being awakened, will produce howls of laughter.

65.　Toss your wallet upon the floor, and tell the subject that it is full of money and he can have it if he can pick it up, but that he cannot do so because his legs are too stiff.

66.　Tell a subject as a posthypnotic that a candy bar will taste like gasoline when he bites into it. Awaken the subject and show a bar of candy. Have a girl take a bite of it, and ask her how it tastes. She will say, "Fine." Give the bar to the subject to bite into. What a reaction!

67.　Hand a subject an empty bottle to hold by its neck. Tell him that it is stuck to his hand and that he cannot drop it no matter how hard he tries.

68.　Tell a subject as a posthypnotic, that he will discover that his nose is made of rubber and will have a lot of fun stretching it out and letting it snap back to his face over and over. Awaken him and leave this subject seated over towards the side of the stage, and he will keep stretching his nose and let it snap back all during the show. Allow the stunt to continue for awhile until you have got lots of laughs out of it, then end it by returning the subject to "sleep."

69.　Have the subjects play "paddy-cake, paddy-cake," as they clap hands with each other. Tell them they are "paddy-caking" faster and faster, and that they cannot stop until you shout, "Stop!"

70.　Here is an old classic that for laughs is hard to beat. Hypnotize one subject and tell him that he is a mother and you will place her baby on her lap, and she will rock it to sleep. Hypnotize another subject and tell him he is the squawking baby. Seat the "baby" on the "mother" and watch the fun. You can, also, give the "mother" a baby bottle to feed the "baby," if you wish.

Needless to say a stunt of this nature should only be used when everyone is in the mood for rollicking fun. Always be careful not to embarrass or belittle anyone.

71.　Tell the hypnotized subject that he is a famous western movie star who is going for a ride on his trusty horse. Seat him backwards in a chair so he is facing the back, as you suggest that he is riding off at a gallop.

72.　The "Horse Race Test" is a riot. Each subject is given a number on their horse in the race and are told that each has bet all their money on their horse. On command, the race starts and subjects are to cheer their horse on as each number is called. Start the race with all of the subjects watching and call out the number of the different horses as each takes the lead. Each time you do, the subject cheers on the horse of his number to be a winner. At the end of the race, all horses that they had bet on lost the race, and all lose their money. The complete contrast of elation in spurring on their winner to the dejection of losing their money is terrific entertainment. This is a very exciting test, especially if the performer dramatizes it "race track announcer style!"

73. As a posthypnotic, tell the subject that everytime he sees you touch your forehead he will shout out loud, "Cuckoo!" and having done so, will promptly forget what he has said. Awaken the subject and touch your head. His reaction will get a good laugh. This can go on at intervals throughout the entire performance, each time the subject yells out "Cuckoo!" at you, the laughs increase. Poking a bit of fun at yourself is good showmanship.

74. A 3-Ring Circus. Hypnotize three subjects and have them stand in a row in the center of the stage. As a posthypnotic, tell each person that he will perform a specific act upon awakening. One is to tie and untie his necktie; the second person is to keep combing his hair; the third subject is to keep buttoning and unbuttoning his shirt. When all three subjects are doing something at the same time, it will have your audiences in stiches. It is amazing how such simple acts as these performed by hypnotized subjects can produce such laughs and response from an audience, but it is true. Such is one of the real marvels of the hypnotic show as entertainment.

75. Odd and Even Hypnotic Experiments. Label all subject on the stage ODD and EVEN, and tell them to remember which they are. In the course of presenting a group test, you can call out that all of the ODD subjects will do such and such and that the EVEN subjects will do such and such. Here are examples:

Odd subjects become hot while Even subject become cold.

Odd subjects laugh while Even subjects cry.

Odd subjects are Republicans while Even subjects are Democrats.

The "Odd and Even Handling" can be used at the very beginning of the hypnotism show. With the committee seated on stage, starting at the right hand side, have each person call out their number, i.e., the first person is one, second is two, thrid is three, and so on. Each person is then asked to remember their number throughout the entire show. Subjects are then hypnotized and the show progresses. You are thus all set to use "Odd and Even Handling" anytime you wish. All you have to say is, "All persons with *odd numbers* will do such and such, and those with *even numbers* will do such and such."

There is good psychology in this handling also, as it gets the group of subjects involved in taking instructions – right from the very start of the show – from the performer. Likewise, it gives them something to turn their attention to as they must *remember* their number. This identifying number can be used in additional ways by simply stating, "Subject number so and so will do this and that, etc." The subjects being designated by numbers gives you ready access to use whatever subject or subjects you wish for the performance of different tests, as all you have to do is to call out the number(s) of the person or persons wanted.

19
Special
Hypnotism Effects

In this chapter, I will provide you with a number of hypnotic novelties which you can include in your programs. These effects are all unusual, and will add to your reputation as a hypnotist.

Hypnotizing Animals

Hypnosis in animals is more a physical condition that it is mental; it resembles catatonia. However as the process renders the animal immobile and it appears asleep, it passes as hypnosis with the audience. Let's just call it "animal hypnotism." You will find hypnotizing animals provides an excellent entertainment segment to include in your show, and the effects are greatly appreciated by the spectators.

To hypnotize a FROG or a LIZARD, flop it over on its back and hold it immobile for a few second. Then carefully remove your hand, and the amimal will remain exactly as you left it — seemingly sleeping. See Fig. 54.

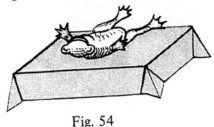

Fig. 54

To remove the condition, snap your fingers for effect beside the animal's head, and quickly flop it over right side up. It will instantly reawaken and move about.

To hypnotize a LOBSTER, stand it up on its head, using its claws as supports, as shown in Fig. 55. Hold it in this position for a few moments, and it will go immediately to "sleep." To remove the condition, merely set it again on its legs.

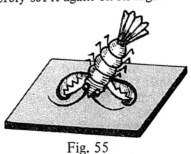

Fig. 55

To hypnotize a CHICKEN, catch hold of the bird by its neck, and force the hen's head down so it lies flat on the table. Then, with a piece of chalk draw a line directly out from its beak for about two feet. See Fig 56.

Fig. 56

Now, carefully remove your hands and it will stay in that exact position motionless. To awaken the chicken, clap your hands loudly beside it, and push its head a bit away from the chalk line.

To hypnotize a GUINEA PIG, first roll the animal over and over a few times on the table, and then lay it on its back. The guinea pig will remain quiescent as if asleep as shown in Fig. 57.

Fig. 57

To awaken the Guinea Pig, blow on its nose and return it to its feet.

To hypnotize a RABBIT, lay it on its back, part its ears with the fingers of your right hand flat on the table, and push its hind legs down to the table with your left hand. See Fig. 58.

Fig. 58

Hold the Rabbit in this stretched out position *on its back,* restricting its movement for about thirty seconds, and then carefully remove your hands. The rabbit will seem as asleep, lying motionless on its back.

To remove the "Hypnotic influence," blow sharply on its nose and push it over on its side. The rabbit will immediately awaken and scamper about.

170

You can make very effective demonstrations in your hypnotism show using these strange animal hypnosis feats. Present them with showmanship by giving suggestions of sleep to the animals combined with mysterious hypnotic passes as you maniuplate them, and they will create very striking effect which the spectators will long remember.

The Hypnotic Wand

I have found this an effective prop to use in the hypnotic show. It appears dramatic, also it can be utilized in a hypnotizing method.

At a plastic supply house, get a two foot length of one half inch diameter lucite rod. This forms the wand. It is attractive and catches the lights on stage. I use it in pointing at the subjects in performing various hypnotic stunts. It looks mysterious and captures audience interest. Also it is effective in waving before the group as you return them to hypnosis in parts of your show, and here it how to use it to hypnotize a solo subject:

Having seen you use "the hypnotic wand" in pointing up many of your demonstrations, your subjects will come to associate it with being hypnotized. Bring a subject forward from the group and have him stand facing you. Tell him that you are going to hypnotize him using the wand.

Have the subject stand erect with his hands by his sides, then ask him to relax just a bit as he focuses his eyes on the tip of one end of the wand, explaining that he is to keep his eyes riveted on that end of the wand at all times and to follow it wherever you move it. Hold the wand in your right hand about eight inches from his face directly on the level of his eyes, and grip the back of his head firmly with your left hand. See Fig. 59.

Now move the wand upward in a slow arc, as shown in Fig. 60. Since you are holding the subject's head rigidly so that it cannot move, only his eyes will turn upward, and when they reach a point where the pupil is almost hidden behind the upper lid, they will suddenly blink shut. At this point, bring the wand down again level with his eyes, and repeat this up and down motion with the wand ten times. At the end of the tenth time when his eye blink shut, tell him to keep his eyes shut tight.

Now place the wand so it touches the center of the top of his head, and tell him to roll his eyes upward under the closed lids as though he were looking back into his head towards the very spot where the wand is touching. Tell him to keep looking upward as you press the wand firmly against the top of his head, and suggest that his eyelids are becoming stuck so tightly together by the power of the wand that he cannot open them, try as hard as he will. Keep a series of such suggestions going directly into his ear, associating his responses as being due to the properties in the hypnotic wand.

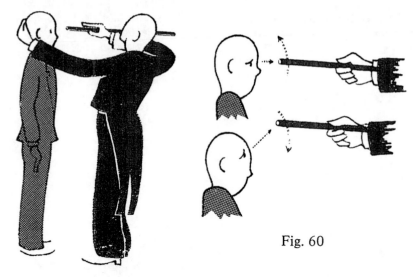

Fig. 60

Fig. 59

As you perform this eyelid fastening technique, move your left hand down from the back of the subject's head and press inward at the nape of his neck at the top of the spinal column. See Fig. 61.

Fig. 61

Press in firmly on the nape of his neck. This produces a deadening sensation through his entire body, and once his eyes have proved themselves fastened and resisting all his efforts to open them, follow on into "the sleep formula," i.e., "Now the hypnotic wand is making you very sleepy. Its power is seeping into your being and is making you go sound alseep in hypnosis right on your feet. Go to sleep, go sound asleep now." The subject will soon be entranced in hypnosis.

172

Hypnotizing With Mechanical Devices

These devices will prove very effective in stage demonstrations of hypnotism. They capture the imagination of the spectators making it both easier to induce hypnosis and add interest and spectacle to the show.

HYPNOTIZING WITH A FLASHLIGHT - THE AFTER-IMAGE TECHNIQUE. My friend, Charles Cook developed this interesting method of hypnotizing employing a pocket Penlite.

In this technique, the subject is seated facing you in readiness for hypnosis. Your lean forward and place the palm of your left hand over his right eye and shine the Penlight directly into his left eye, holding the light about an inch from the eye, as shown in Fig. 62.

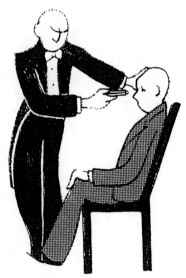

Fig. 62

A pocket Penlight is not powerful and being a dim light will not bother his eyes. Tell the subject to keep staring into the light, to relax his body completely. After about thrity seconds, command him to close his eyes tightly together. Owing to the light which has been directed in his eye, he will now experience a very vivid *after-image,* and this sensation you describe to him as a hypnotic technique, thus:

"You will see inside your closed lids a very bright spot of light. This spot will change in color as you watch it. It will fade away altogether, and then it will reappear. Watch closely this spot. Concentrate your complete attention upon this spot. And, as you watch it, you will begin to feel yourself getting very drowsy and sleepy."

Continue on with "the sleep formula" and the process of hypnotizing, and soon your subject will be in deep hypnosis.

You will find this method of hypnotizing very effective; what makes it particularly unique is that the after-image in the subject's own eye is used as the "fixation object" rather than an external point. The method will swiftly produce results.

HYPNOTIZING WITH HYPNOGRAPH BUTTONS. You can design these "buttons" yourself: Trace Fig 63. on paper and mount on cardboard. Then fill in the black portion with india ink. Cut around the outline, and you have made a "hypnograph button." Make a number of these small discs.

Hand a "hypnograph button" to each members of your committee, and have them hold it up in front of their eyes and center their gaze on the central white circle, as shown in Fig. 64.

Fig. 63

Fig. 64

Use these special discs as the "fixation object," and proceed to hypnotize the subjects giving suggestions of "the hypnograph" becoming blurred before their eyes, eyelids getting heavy, etc., and then when all eyes close that their hands supporting it are becoming heavy and falling to their laps. When all hands fall proceed into the "sleep formula" inducing complete hypnosis. This is a very good stage method to use in hypnotizing the entire committee.

HYPNOTIZING WITH THE HYPNOTIC SPIRAL. This is a popular mechanical method. It consists of a cardboard disc designed as a black and white spiral. The disc is mounted in connection with a motor so it may be revolved around and around. The effect produced is decidedly hypnotic. See Fig. 65.

In using the device, "the hypnotic spiral" is placed before the subject and the motor turned on which revolves the disc. The swirling spiral is tremendously compelling and rapidly induces hypnosis as the subject stares at it. It may be used on the stage directed toward the committee in hypnotizing the group.

Likewise "the hypnotic spiral" is effective in hypnotizing a solo subject. I have designed my disc mounted on a stand so it may be elevated before the eyes of the seated subject who has to stare up at it. See Fig. 66.

Fig. 65

Fig. 66

For this operation, set the disc about six inches from the eyes of the subject, and instruct him to stare at it while it revolves for as long as he can keep his eyes open. Then start the disc rotating and apply your favorite hypnotic method. The effect of this machine is powerful and will hypnotize rapidly many of the most difficult subjects.

Instantaneous Hypnosis

Unquestionably the most certain way to achieve instantaneous hypnosis is to first hypnotize the subject by a slower method, and while he is in trance give him a posthypnotic suggestion that whenever you speak a certain word or make a certain gesture that he will *instantly* go to sleep again in hypnosis. This developes a "cue response," and when the awakened subject sees the cue, he immediately reenters the hypnotic state.

Witnessing the hypnotic so react to the posthypnotic suggestion of instantaneous hypnosis is very impressive.

Also, there are other ways of speed hypnosis which hypnotize quickly. *These methods are called unexpected hypnosis.* Here are a couple of effective techniques:

1. THE POSTURE SWAYING METHOD. In performing the test of pulling a subject over backwards, if he responds readily, as he falls back into your arms, suddenly and forcefully suggest, "Keep your eyes closed, closed tightly and go to sleep! Go sound, sound

to sleep this instant!" In many cases, the subject stimulated by wonder and bewilderment at his response in "The Falling Test" will instantly pass into hypnosis.

2. THE HAND LOCKING METHOD. Having locked your subject's hands tightly together so he cannot unclasp them, and while he is straining to take them apart, rather than releasing his hands ask him to look directly into your eyes, and you suggest, "Your hands are stuck and they will not come apart. Now your eyes too are getting heavy, the lids are closing and they, too, will get stuck tightly together. So tightly that you cannot open them anymore than you can take your stuck hands apart. Close your eyes. Close them tight. The lids are stuck, stuck! You cannot open them try as hard as you will. (The subject tries in vain to open his fastened eyelids.) Now forget all about your eyes, forget all about your hands. Your stuck hands are relaxing and coming apart. Your arms and hands are falling to your sides, and by the time they reach your sides you will be sound asleep. SLEEP!" Follow this preliminary directly into "the sleep formula" inducing deep hypnosis. This method is very effective for rapidly producing hypnosis directly from a test in waking suggestion.

These methods of "unexpected hypnosis," while not usable in all situations, when applied at the right time and with the right subjects, are among the fastest methods of hypnotizing known.

THE CRYSTAL BALL METHOD OF HYPNOTIZING. This method is related to "The Hypnotic Wand" technique which you have previously studied, as it attaches as mystical significance to some object as having a degree of power to which the subject will respond. In this handling, the legendary crystal ball is used for that purpose.

Introduce this as an experiment at a social entertainment. People are very interested in psychical things, and your crystal ball will create much interest. Select a subject who shows a sincere interest in ESP, and tell him of the uses of the crystal by mystics for scrying, and stress how many people claim that a crystal ball exerts a subtle influence over them which develops psychic powers. This description is suggestive in effect, and aim your suggestions so the subject feels privileged at being able to work with your crystal in an experiment in psychic influence which you propose; an experiment in which you suggest that he perform as a medium and enter trance.

Next explain to the subject exactly how he is to use the crystal for this purpose, viz., he is to place it on a table in front of himself, sit back comfortably in a chair and center his eyes on it. See Fig. 67.

He is to gaze directly at the ball, on past the reflections on is surface and into its very depths. Explain that if he is doing the experiment correctly the crystal will gradually appear to become

Fig. 67

darker and a sort of milky mist will form in front of his eyes. This mist will seem to grow and expand until it entirely engulfs him. He is then to let his mind float out in this mist, as it were, until blackness envelopes him. And with the blackness will come a state of mediumistic entrancement.

In this experiment, do not mention either sleep or hypnotism; keep your suggestions entirely centered on the subject's desire to arouse his own psychic powers.

When all is understood and your subject is in an eager mood to try the experiment of entrancing himself by making use of your remarkable crystal ball, have him enter alone a semi-darkened room, and close the door. Thus alone he performs the experiment exactly as you have instructed.

After a period of about twenty minutes, you enter the room softly, and in many instances you will find the subject seated in the chair with his eyes closed, or else staring blankly into space -- entranced. Speak to him quietly, and if he answers without being disturbed, you can swiftly bring him under hypnotic control.

Extra Sensory Perception Experiments in Hypnotism

The method of hypnotizing just described using the crystal ball is excellent for experimenting with tests of the type which will now be described. For experimenting with the more subtle abilities of the mind via, hypnosis, better results will often be obtained if the trance is induced in a manner which will stimulate the psychic talents rather than by using suggestions of sleep. This is psychologically to be expected as the hypnotic is extremely responsive to suggestions and will react accordingly. In this instance, the suggestions have been directed towards ESP.

The special hypnotism effects which I will now give you are especially suitable to social entertaining. Here are three tests which are remarkable:

PSYCHIC TEST ONE. Take five playing cards, mix them, and lay them face downward on the table. Bring forward your

177

hypnotized subject, place the palm of his hand on the back of one of the cards, and command him to name it. He will do so, and you can check on the correctness by lifting up the card so all can see. Repeat the test several times.

PSYCHIC TEST TWO. Take a hat and collect a number of articles from about ten different spectators. Have the spectators drop the articles in the hat themselves, and do not touch them yourself. Then give the hat to the subject and command him to pick up each article in turn and take it back to its owners. Some subjects will start right out, others you will have to encourage by taking their hand and going along with them. But once he gets started, the subject will experience little difficulty in returning all of the objects correctly.

PSYCHIC TEST THREE. Try now an experiment in telepathic hypnotism. Suggest to the hypnotic that his mind is clear of all thoughts, and that he is to visualize the room in which he is performing with his eyes closed. Tell him he can see you easily, can see the spectators, and is acutely aware of everything which is going on about him. Then suggest that you are going to send mental directions to him of various things he is to perform via telepathy. Explain that his instructions will come in the form of mental pictures in his mind, and that he is to do exactly as the pictures direct.

Then go into the audience and have different spectators whisper different tests they would like the hypnotic to perform, such as go to the blackboard and make a mark, remove his right shoe, take off his coat, etc. Having decided on a specific test, speak to the subject directly, "Ready, I am concentrating. Receive my thought and do as the picture that is forming in your mind directs." In many cases the subject will respond correctly.

Experiments in extra sensory perception are never 100% accurate, results must be tabulated in percentage of accuracy. As always in tests of this nature, the success of the experiment depends upon the subject's innate ESP ability, so results are bound to vary. Your own mental attitude is important also; you must feel confident in your own mind that the subject will respond. Hold an experimental attitude. If the subject succeeds in a test mark it as positive, if he does not succeed mark it as negative, and keep a record.

ESP experiments via hypnotism provide superlative thought-provoking intimate entertainment.

20
Staging
the Hypnotism Show

In this chapter, you will learn how to produce the Hypnotism Show as theatre as we study audience/performer relationship, the presentation of hypnotism on stage, and hypnotic stagecraft.

THE 20th CENTURY HYPNOTISM SHOW. Hypnotism is a venerable art. It was ancient in the times of early Egypt when the pyramids were built. During its long history it has gone through many phases, and today stands at its zenith as a tool in the arsenal of the physician to aid mankind. As such it is useful, remarkable and scientific, and it is the duty of the stage hypnotist to promote those qualities. Not that you should make your presentation dry and academic, as in stage hypnotism *entertainment is the thing.* Indeed, comedy and drama are your properties to convey your message, but underlying your show there must be a sincere respect for both the art and the science of hypnotism. Such is the purpose of the 20th century hypnotism show.

The basic theme of the old fashioned hypnotic show was to exhault the performer as a sort of mastermind who dominated the will of all he approached, and to prove his great powers his victims were caused to perform all manner of ridiculous stunts. Thus the programming of the show was designed to heap imagined glory on the hypnotist and ridicule on the subjects.

As I have stressed in this text, the modern approach to the hypnotic entertainment is very different from the above, it now being the aim of the performer to heap glory on the phenomena, itself, and his subjects' abilities to perform such. The hypnotist, himself, assumes the role of instructor. There is sound psychology in such an approach that completely revolutionizes the hypnotism show from its antiquated predecessor, modernizes it to meet present day demands for entertainment, elevates the serious side of its usefulness in the fields of medicine and psychology, and lifts it to the height of art.

THE PRESENTATION OF STAGE HYPNOTISM. Every performer has his own style of working. Some will hypnotize with smooth persuasive techniques, while others will utilize more aggressive methods. And specific routines too, and the variety of effects presented, will vary with the individual entertainer, but underlying the entire presentation of your hypnotic show always incorporate these six fundamental rules:

Rule No. 1. *Never try to be a comedian.* Hypnotism from the point-of-view of the performer must be essentially a dignified and serious business. This does not mean that you are to be glum or

Ormond McGill demonstrates a *Headline Prediction* effect for members of the Honolulu Police Department during his "Concert of Hypnotism" Show. Experiments in mental-magic occasionally make a nice introduction to exhibitions of hypnotism as feats of ESP blend excellently with hypnosis, as both are regarded as the magic of the mind.

stodgy in your presentation. In fact, be lively and dynamic. But deliberate jokes and attempts to be funny have no place in the presentation of stage hypnotism. Let all of your humor come from the hypnotic situations evolved.

Rule No. 2. *Never ridicule your subjects.* Remember, your committee is composed of volunteers from the audience itself, and to ridicule them is the same as ridiculing your audience -- which is entertainment suicide. People like people and what makes the hypnotism show truly great entertainment is the human interest factor. Always treat your subjects with the utmost in courtesy and respect. While some of your effects may be extremely funny, always make them serve the end in your presentation of illustrating some hypnotic or psychological principle; not to make the subjects appear ridiculous.

Rule No. 3. *Incorporate science in your presentation.* The exact degree to which you can do this depends upon your personality as an entertainer and the type of audiences to which you perform. But always, to some extent, keep an element of scientific experimentation in your hypnotic work.

Rule No. 4. *Take your audience honestly into your confidence.* Hypnotism has for a long enough time been shrouded in mystery and a residue still remains. With the modern understanding of the subject you can well afford to frankly discuss its phenomena. For example, don't be afraid to place the credit for hypnotic occurrences where it belongs -- to the minds of the subjects themselves. Don't be afraid to admit that you have no especial powers over the minds of your subjects. Don't be afraid to explain that the underlying principles of hypnotism are the working of psychological laws without a vestige of the supernatural.

You will find that honest frankness about hypnotism far from destroying your prestige in the eyes of the audience will elevate it immensely. People, nowadays, like to consider themselves intelligent enough to consider scientific matters, and the facts of science related to the operation of the human mind holds tremendous fascination for everyone. As for reducing the mystery of hypnotism by explaining the true facts: do you reduce the wonders of electricity by explaining the things it can do? Conversely you increase its wonders. So it is with hypnotism. The more you explain of its wonders the deeper the wonder you produce, for the human mind will always be the greatest mystery of all.

Rule No. 5. *Interest your committee.* As a hypnotist you have one factor which is completely different from conventional theatre; all of your "props" are human. You must therefore hold the interest of those "props" (your subjects) throughout the entire performance. To such ends, your presentation as a hypnotist becomes a dual process which much include your committee as well as your audience.

Rule No. 6. *Always entertain.* Constantly bear in mind that your foremost purpose as a stage performer is to entertain the audience. One can readily become so wrapped up in the subject matter of hypnosis that it is easy to slip into the mistake of experimenting with things that entertain yourself and hold little interest to the spectators. Make everything you do convey a message and have a purpose. Make every effect in your show have entertainment value. No matter how intellectual and scientific your performance may be, remember its value as theatre is nil unless it is also entertaining.

And most important of all, design your entire show to bring a pleasure response to both the spectators and the subjects. Create all tests so they are relaxing and pleasant, then everyone will enjoy your show and profit from it.

Your thorough mastery of hypnotic techniques, your development of a smoothly routined hypnotic show, and your incorporation of these six rules spell success in establishing your audience/performer relationship and your presentation of stage hypnotism.

PLANNING PATTER FOR THE HYPNOTISM SHOW. Closely related to presentation is patter. Patter is the *on stage talk* you use in presenting your program. In this text, I have carefully given you much of the patter that I use in my own shows. You will note that the patter used in the hypnotism show encompasses the variuos "suggestion formulas" in which certain key words, as, "now," "all right," "sleep," "count of three," etc. are used frequently. In print such seem repetitious, but in performance these verbal exclamations function to establish "a call to action." Naturally each performer will employ such as is suited to his particular style of presentation.

Planning patter is highly individual, so each performer must develop his own as befits his personality. In general, make your patter up-to-date, lightly scientific, praising to the important uses of hypnotism in medical and psychological fields, and pleasantly conversational in nature.

DEVELOPING YOUR ORIGINAL SHOW. Now that you have the "know how" of hypnotism and the types of phenomena you can produce, the variety of effects and combinations of effects you can create are numberless. It is in this creative end of developing your own hypnotic entertainment that you can show your individualism and originality.

By way of illustration, let us consider the development of a test based around a posthypnotic negative hallucination:

This test might be called "The Invisible Hypnotist," and in its dramatic design the subject is hypnotized and given the posthypnotic suggestion that when he awakens he will be perfectly normal in all ways, *except* that he will not be able to see you. He will be able to see everyone and everything else, and even able to hear and feel you, but he cannot see you at all; you are absolutely invisible to him, until such time as you remove the suggestion with a snap of your fingers beside his ear.

Then awaken the subject from hypnosis.

The subject's reaction you can imagine as he looks vainly about trying to find you, his surprise at hearing your voice or feeling your touch while you are invisible, and then comes the climax when you suddenly materialize before his eyes with a snap of your fingers.

You can appreciate the high entertainment value of orginizations of tests such as this one which you create for your show. Another example using the invisible theme we might call "The Dancing Handerchief."

Hypnotize your subject and give him the posthypnotic suggestion that when he awakens he will be perfectly normal in all ways, but that he will see a handkerchief dancing about the stage entirely under it own power. Look as closely as he will he will not see any person or anything holding it up and moving it about. It appears to be dancing by magic.

Then awaken the subject, and have someone take a handkerchief by a corner and dance it about the stage. A strange thing will happen, the moment the person takes hold of the handkerchief he disappears to the subject, and the handkerchief seemingly becomes motivated by itself.

In these examples, you will observe we have the operation of the indentical hypnotic phenomena, yet from the audience's point-of-view each effect is entirely different. Use this principle for originating your own effects. Thought and ingenuity on your part can make the production aspects of your hypnotic show amazingly original.

MAKE YOUR HYPNOTIC PHENOMENA VISUAL. Good show production calls for making all of your hypnotic effects visual to the audience. No matter how profound the hypnosis you induce, there would be little entertainment value in observing a subject witnessing an hallucination unless he responds to that hallucination with action.

To emphasize this point, note the contrast in audience enjoyment of an effect in these two handlings:

Having hypnotized your subject you tell him that when he opens his eyes he will see a cat on the floor. The subject sees the hallucination, but "so what" as far as the audience is concerned.

The entertainer would handle the experiment this way, and create a sensation, viz., it is suggested to the subject, "When you open your eyes you will see a cat on the floor, it will rub itself against your leg. You will try to kick it away but it won't go away, so you will have to pick it up in your lap and stroke it to keep it still."

The increase in the entertainment value of the second handling is obvious. *Remember, as a creative performer to make it your rule to establish and produce in all of your hypnotic tests a dramatic action response so that the audience can visually follow the experiment and be entertained by its effect.*

EMPHASIZE YOUR HYPNOTIC EFFECTS. You can also greatly increase the entertainment value of your effects if you will amplify the subject's reaction by your showmanship in exhibiting those reactions. By way of illustration, let's suppose you have posthypnotically suggested to a subject that when he awakens from the trance he will find himself in a totally dark room and will not be able to see anything, and that he will grope his way about the stage in inky darkness until you tell him that the lights have been turned on. You can appreciate how such an effect can be amplified by having other members of the committee wave their hands in front of the subject as he gropes about in the "darkness," or by your dramatically passing a lighted match before his eyes which he totally fails to see.

Of such devices the showmanship of hypnotism is born.

SPEED AND TIME IN THE HYPNOTISM SHOW. Every device you can create to add the pace of your hypnotic show should be employed and will increase its entertainment value. To such ends, utilizing the principle of posthypnosis by suggesting to each subject that the next time you hypnotize him he will immediately drop into hypnosis will greatly speed up your induction processes.

And give consideration to "the playing time" of your overal show. Hypnotism offers such a tremendous scope of emotions that too much hypnosis at one time rather exhausts an audience. Keep yourself alert in watching your audience's reactions, and when you feel that the spectators have seen enough, always wind up your show. A show of approximately an hour's length (more or less) is ample for demonstrations of hypnosis. While a full evening's performance of hypnotism may be given, generally your program will hold more entertainment appeal if you balance the show with other related demonstrations such as a feats with memory, conjuring, mental-magic, or whatever you wish. Also a musical interlude fits in well with a hypnotic program. Conversely, it is doubtful if a really convincing demonstration of hypnotism can be presented in less than thirty minutes.

WOMAN'S PLACE IN HYPNOTISM. Time was when only men were regarded as hypnotists, but such is no longer the case. Women have entered successfully most every field that men have, and hypnotism is no exception. Joan Brandon started the trend, to be followed by the widely acclaimed Pat Collins, Ginger Court, and others who have become expert hypnotists.

PROGRAMMING YOUR HYPNOTIC ENTERTAINMENT. No matter what precise effects you use or what length of program you plan, the modern hypnotism show most frequently follows the pattern as here presented. You can use this outline in developing your own hypnotic entertainments:

INTRODUCTION

OPENING LECTURE

COMMITTEE INVITATION

FIRST TEST WITH ENTIRE GROUP

EXPERIMENTS IN WAKING SUGGESTION

INDIVIDUAL EXAMPLE OF HYPNOTISM

GROUP HYPNOSIS

EXPERIMENTS IN HYPNOTIC SUGGESTION

THE CLIMAX OF THE SHOW

CONCLUSION

The exact length of time which will be given to each segment of this pattern depends entirely upon the exact show you are preparing. But for the hypnotism show to be successful and acceptable always construct in a semblance of the foregoing sequence.

To sum up the presentation of hypnotism as entertainment it can be said that a show of this nature must be dramatically produced to reveal the wonders of the human mind through graphic experiments, humorous incidents, scientific explanations, and thought-provoking phenomena

Hypnotic Stagecraft

While the hypnotism show may be effectively presented without "props" of any kind other than some awaiting chairs for the committee, there are simple ways to dress it up and build the show into real theatre. Here are various devices in this regard which I have found effective in my international performances:

THE CHAIRS. At an entertainment of hypnotism, the first thing an audiences sees on stage is a group of chairs. As such, it logically follows that the nicer the appearance of these chairs the nicer the appearance of your stage setting. A straggly group of chairs of a variety of sizes and types is quite a contrast to a neat and orderly row of identical chairs. Then, too, you are shortly going to invite volunteers to come forward and sit in those chairs, so it is important to have them look inviting to the forthcoming committee members.

The exact type of chairs you use is immaterial, but an armless, straight-back type works best. Folding chairs are practical and strong. If possible have them all uniform in type and in good condition. While usually the chairs used in the hypnotism show are obtained from the place where the show is being given, if the performer really wishes to stage his show in ultra fashion, what could be neater than a row of chrome plated chairs with black seat and back rest, and with rubber stops on each leg so they won't slide.

If you use a large number of chairs on stage (twenty or so) arrange them in a semicircle, starting near the first wing on each side of the stage, as shown in Fig. 68.

If no more than a dozen chairs are used, then you can place them in a straight row in the center of the stage. Place the chairs about eight inches apart, so that while the subjects will be seated closely together in a group, they will not touch each other.

It is well, in addition to the committee chairs, to have one special chair that you set apart and use for the individual tests. This chair can be larger in size and more comfortable, if you wish. Make it seem as though when one sits in this special chair that something very special is going to happen.

THE CURTAINS. Most hypnotists make use of whatever curtains they find in the place of performance, but if you have any choice in the matter, or if you carry a curtain of your own to hang, black, blue, or rich wine colored curtains are fine and add a touch of elegance to your stage. There are folding curtain stands on the market which make it possible to support small 6' x 6' curtains. These are portable and assemble quickly. Two or three of these placed on stage add to the decoration.

THE LIGHTS. Many hypnotists work in full-up stage lights. When there is an opportunity to do so however, some light changes will add drama to your show. Things of this nature are what gives your show theatre value. If you have the advantage of good lighting by all means take advantage of it. An effective light handling for the hypnotism show is to use red and blue foots and borders on stage for your opening remarks, and work in a white spot. This gives a quality of depth to the appearance of your stage, and concentrates the attention of the spectators upon you as the star of the show.

As you invite the subjects on stage, bring the stage lights full up and turn on the house lights. Once your committee is seated, turn out the house lights, but leave stage lights full up for your first group test.

From here on through the show, your lighting pattern is stage red and blues for each individual test with a solo subject, and full up for all group tests. *Give your spotlight man instructions to follow you with a white spot at all times.*

Below are listed some special lighting effects that fit in well to the hypnotism show and add glamour, viz.:

Have a baby spot mounted overhead in the grids. Arrange an amber gelatine over the lens and focus it vertically downward directly on your special hypnotic chair near stage center. See Fig. 69.

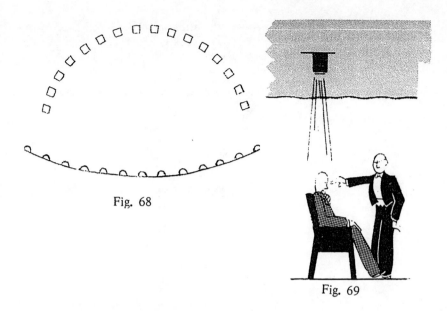

Fig. 68

Fig. 69

A baby spot in the wings focused at the performer's face is also very effective. Use a colored gelatine in front of the lens, or a color wheel can be used on this spotlight to good advantage. See Fig. 70.

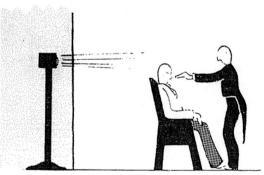

Fig. 70

In the event that you cannot conveniently arrange for such a baby spot, as described above, a floor lamp placed behind the subject's chair and directed over his shoulder towards the performer will give an interesting, informal lighting effect. See Fig. 71.

A double-faced mirror mounted upright on a revolving turntable with a baby spotlight focused on it gives a most hypnotic effect as it revolves. Place this device behind the first curtain wing, and as it revolves the mirrors reflect out flashes of light about the stage. See. Fig. 72. This is especially effective to use while hypnotizing a solo subject.

Fig. 71

Fig. 72

Lighting techniques such as these enrich the hypnotism show, make it more spectacular, and take the hypnotic effects over the footlights right to the spectators themselves. Colored lights, also, have definite psychological effects on hypnotic subjects, so remember these principles and use them in staging your hypnotic show:

Yellow light increases the subject's suggestibility, while purple and blue lights are sleep inducing. You can apply these affects to your stage hypnotism show by arranging a lamp with two bulbs placed so it will shine directly on the face of the subject, as shown in Fig. 73.

When you first commence to hypnotize the subject, switch on the *yellow light*. Then as his eyes close and you follow on into "the sleep formula" switch off the yellow and turn on *the purple or blue light*. You will find the use of these colored lights dramatic and effective in hypnotizing.

HYPNOTIC TRICKS-OF-THE-TRADE. In addition to colored lights, there are several other devices that aid in hypnotizing. Before beginning a show, I find it a good idea to stand backstage and imagine that I am charging my hands with "hypnotic force." To do this, stand erect and breathe deeply. Then tense up your fingers, turn the hands palms towards each other and hold them with the fingertips about two inches apart.

Fig. 73

Now imagine that you can feel an electric-like current passing down your arms and is flowing out of your fingertips to "spark" across to each other. Strangely, as you practice this you will actually experience a tingling sensation in your fingers. I find it a good metal-set for a stimulating performance. Get the sensation going strongly in your hands, then walk out briskly and start the show.

For a mysterious gaze in hypnotizing on stage, focus your eyes at a point on the level of the eyes of your subject *about six inches in back of his head*. This gives the appearance that each of your eyes is staring directly into his, looking within his very brain, and is extremely effective in holding attention. This is another variation of "the hypnotic gaze."

A simple device known as Chevreul's Pendulum may be effectively used in the hypnotism show to illustrate the operation

189

of suggestion. This may be easily made merely by trying a finger ring to a length of thread (or any type of weight such as a fishing sinker may be used).

Have the subject hold the string between the thumb and forefinger of his right hand, allowing the weight to dangle free, as shown in Fig. 74. Request him to hold the dangling weight as still as he can, and then suggest that he think to himself of it commencing to swing from right to left back and forth. Keep the idea of it swinging back and forth over and over, and in a few moments the weight will actually commence swinging back and forth, back and forth, directly in response to his thoughts.

Fig. 74

Now, have your subject change his thought to the idea of the weight commencing to swing around and around in a circle. In direct response to that thought, the pendulum will stop its back and forth path, and will swing in a wide circle.

As a stage demonstration, each person in the committee can be given a pendulum, and all work it together as a group.

Odors, also, have their place in the hypnotic show and increase suggestibility. If you have a girl assistant, have her wear a potent oriental perfume. And a pot or two of incense burning on each side of the stage has its purpose. Devices such as these lend atmosphere to the hypnotism show, and increase the anticipation of both committee members and the audience.

ASSISTANTS IN THE SHOW. Although the hypnotic show can be handled strictly on a one-man show basis, if you do have assistants they can increase the show's production value. Your assistants can bring in various "props" to you as you need them, also they can usher the volunteers to seats as they come onto the stage. One or two assistants at most are all you will ever need for the hypnotism show, and keep them unobtrusively in the background. A boy assistant can wear a tuxedo and girls be in evening gowns. Avoid flashy costumes, for in the hypnotic show dignity is the motif.

THE PERFORMER'S DRESS. The hypnotist presenting a formal stage show will find "tails" very appropriate. However, some people can wear them well and others cannot. If you are among the latter, then black tuxedo trousers and a brocaded dinner jacket makes an effective dress.

For programs of a lecture or social type, a neat business suit is splendid. Dress well. Good clothes increase prestige, and in hypnotism prestige goes a long ways.

THE PUBLIC ADDRESS SYSTEM AND MUSIC. The use of a P.A. system is an essential to the modern hypnotic show. People expect it for easy listening, and the mike forms the very heart of your performing. When the show first starts, there is the mike in center stage ready for your introduction, opening lecture, and on into the show. And you can take the mike with you as you perform your different tests. Your audience will thus be able to clearly hear you and understand exactly what is going on at all times.

Likewise the use of a microphone is important in making your voice more commanding. Especially when working with the entire committee as a group is it vital, as everyone of your subjects through the P.A. speaker can clearly hear you and follow your suggestions. *The professional use of the microphone is your secret for holding the attention of your subjects and your audience at one and the same time.*

Background music is very helpful in putting theatre into the hypnotism show. If you have an orchestra or organist with which to work you can get some wonderful effects, but for most shows the use of records or tape cassettes played over the P.A. system works nicely.

The essential thing in selecting suitable hypnotic music is to use pieces that are not too well known and that are soothing rather than arousing. You wish to establish mood, and for this prupose organ or symphonic selections are usually best. Get pieces that suggest sleep, dreams, or moods of quiet and rest, and make certain that the music maintains the same sound level throughout the numbers. Having selected the music you like, apply it to these spots in your show:

Before the Show: use a dramatic symphonic piece as overture.

As the Subject Comes to the Stage: use a smooth piece with a bit of lively rhythm to encourage marching up onto the stage.

For the Initial Group Experiment Establishing the Hypnotic Mood: use soft dreamy music.

For Hypnotizing the Entire Committee: use soft, sleepy mood music.

You will find that the use of music throughout your show adds greatly to its charm, and also increases your control over the subject, and makes hypnotizing easier. Always keep the volume down so the music forms a melodious background to your speech and suggestions.

191

Study now the "inner secrets" in the next chapter, and you will soon be ready to entertain with hypnotism.

21
The Inner Secrets
of Stage Hypnotism

The principles considered in this chapter are so basic to the entire field of hypnotism that we are bound to cover some ground already gone over; the application of these secrets is the real key to your success as a stage hypnotist in which entertainment is your chief aim, and towards which objective all your efforts should be directed. I will go over these factors with you point by point.

Expectancy

Here lies one of the great secrets of successful stage hypnotism -- *the expectancy of your subjects on the stage to be hypnotized by you.* Psychologically speaking such is, of course, the real producer of all the phenomena, for if the subjects keenly *expect* to be hypnotized they are *mentally set* to go into hypnosis. Accordingly, every stimuli you present must be aimed to arouse to greater and greater heights this expectancy.

The process commences with your advertising before the subjects even come to the show. It continues to build on through your opening lecture as they come forward to the stage. It developes further as each test is performed, and finally culminates in the complete hypnotizing of the subjects. Since all of these factors are entirely under the control of the operator, the performing of stage hypnotism through the cultivation of the proper expectancy can become extremely successful.

The Stage Situation

Being the star on the stage gives you prestige which is one of the major advantages the stage operator enjoys over any other type of hypnotist. Also there is a certain atmosphere about the stage that is conducive to the successful demonstrating of hypnotism. The lights, the music, the curtains, the tenseness of being on stage, and above all the attention of the audience upon the stage activities are all factors working so powerfully in the performer's favor that hypnotism under such conditions may frequently be more readily accomplished than under any other. *It is because of this "stage situation" that hypnosis can be induced on the stage with greater speed than in any other situation* Also, striking phenomena sometimes produced that are *rarely* seen elsewhere.

The Importance of Importance

Few things are more essential to the stage hypnotist than to act on this phrase, "The Importance of Importance." For the more important you make your work appear the greater will be your success. So observe these three rules: (1) make the state of hypnotism, itself, important; (2) make the audience feel that your performance of hypnotism is important; (3) make your subjects feel that being hypnotized is important.

Towards achieving these objectives, a dignified, semi-scientific approach to presenting the hypnotism show is important.

Social Approval

If you have "sold" your audience completely on hypnosis as a superior mental state of scientific value, you can appreciate the favorable position such will place your subjects. Far from being regarded as weak-willed stooges, as was the case in the old fashioned hypnotism show, your subjects shine upon the stage in the position of experiments with psychological wonders which they are learning how to master.

Aim all of your work towards building social approval for both hypnotism and your subjects entering hypnosis. In direct ratio to the amount of social approval you develop will be your success as a hypnotist.

No Challenge

Your entire presentation must always be to cultivate a response of "no challenge" from both the spectators and the subjects. The perpetuated belief that the hypnotist dominates the weaker wills of his subjects are things you must overcome. Accordingly, you must make sincere efforts to conduct yourself in a manner to convey that there is no challenge to being hypnotized; your attitude is that of the teacher instructing students in the learning of a skill.

Subject Responsibility

Lay the entire proceedings of the show directly in the laps of the subjects themselves, and make them responsible for the show's success. Frankly state the truth that the ability to be hypnotized lies entirely within the subject, and that your part in the process is to assist as expertly as you can to help them obtain hypnosis . . . *then let the subjects assume all of the responsibilities for the results.*

The human factor in hypnotism is bound to bring you face to face with failure occasionally, but you can save yourself from embarrassment in such moments if you are seemingly impersonal about the results obtained. If you succeed in a test be very matter-of-fact about it, and always congratulate the subject (or subjects, as the case may be) letting him take the credit. If a test fails, be equally unconcerned and either repeat the experiment or proceed calmly on to another test. Just keep in mind that if a failure does not bother you that the audience will not be bothered by it either. Further, audiences like things that are difficult and not too easily accomplished.

194

On Taking Bows

Applause in the hypnotism show should always be spontaneous. If the audience gives you an ovation, acknowledge it of course, but never deliberately ask for applause by a bow after each test you perform. Rather proceed directly from one experiment on into the next keeping your show moving along at a professional pace. And don't be disappointed if you don't receive too much applause. Hypnotism is such interesting subject matter that it absorbs the audience's attention to a degree that their interest abstracts them. The favorable after-the-show talk is what measures your success.

Routining the Show

Exactly as is the case with any type of the performing arts, the manner in which you routine your show forms a large factor in its success. To this end, develop a hypnotic routine of effects that seem to produce the best results for you and proves the most entertaining to the audience, then learn that routine throughly and stick to it. A few variations every so often are of course permissable, but for the most part get your patter and presentation so throughly routined that it is second nature to yourself. You have more than enough distractions in holding the audience's interest, the committee's attention, and hypnotizing all at the same time without having the additional concern of having to worry about imperfectly mastered routine as well.

Group Size, Age, and Sex

The number of volunteers you will wish to invite forward to take part in your program will depend upon the type of hypnotism show you are doing. Naturally, a social club show will call for fewer committee members than will a full stage show.

Generally speaking, I never plan to work with less than six subjects or more than twenty-five, and have chairs awaiting for them accordingly. For the stage show, about twenty chairs is ideal and will fill a large stage. The hypnotist must decide pretty much for himself as to how many subjects he likes to work with, some preferring a sizeable group while others find that not over a dozen subjects is best for them.

And in inviting the committee on stage, specify, "No children please. Only persons of high school, college age, or older please volunteer. This is not because children do not make good hypnotic subjects as they are excellent once you capture their imaginations, but in a mixed group a child makes the older members feel self-conscious in responding to suggestions when a child does likewise. *So keep the children off the stage.*

The majority of the volunteers forming your committee will be from the high school and college age group; they make excellent subjects and concentrate well. *Invite both sexes to come forward when you ask for volunteers.* The girls will be a little hesitant at first, but a little coaxing soon gets a number up. *A mixed committee composed of two-thirds men and one-third women is ideal.* Let as many persons as wish come up on stage, and don't send any down just because all of the seats are taken. The volunteers who can't find seats may stand in the rear of the seated group behind the chairs. Having this overflow of potential subjects gives you a natural excuse subsequently to dismiss from the stage any persons who you find uncooperative or undersirable to retain, as you explain at the commencement of the show that obviously you have more subjects than you can possibly use, and while you will give them all an equal chance to participate you will shortly ask some to leave as you wish to especially work with persons on stage who concentrate the best.

Then give them all a preliminary group test, and the subjects who do not respond dismiss at once, until you have all of the chairs filled only with good, potential subjects.

Judging Your Committee

Experience is the best teacher in spotting your best subjects; it's a knack that comes through repeated observation. Generally speaking, your good subjects usually have serious demeanor and have a certain relaxed "look" about them. If close friends sit together they tend to talk to each other, and girls all in a group to giggle, so separate them in the committee spacing them amongst the others. With this handling you will find you can control your group better, and it puts you in the position of being the director of the situation.

Subjects you should avoid and dismiss as promptly as you can diplomatically are the ones who sit down with a cocky, "Now you show me air," and cross their legs, subjects who insist on talking to others in the group, subjects who chew gum and subjects who smoke or smell of alcohol. And beware of the subject with the perpetual grin. *This spotting and judging of potential subjects is one of the first things the stage hypnotists must learn for the smooth staging of the show.*

Group Hypnotism

Group hypnosis is very important to the stage performer for the percentage factor in a group of persons locates for him his desirable subjects. Actually, in some ways it is easier to hypnotize many subjects while working with the entire group that it is individually. A group seems to develop a mutual spirit of cooperation that carries over from one subject to the other until all are responding in unison. It is the psychology of the crowd in operation.

Your rule in handling group hypnotic phenomena is to make it perfectly understood exactly what is expected of the subjects, and give your suggestions clearly. Emphasize your verbal suggestions with visual gestures, as much as possible. Also it is a good policy to sometimes demonstrate the test you intend to work with a single subject before applying it to the group. Seeing the solo subject react, the group immediately understands exactly what reaction is expected of them, and understanding performs successfully.

Progressive Selling

Although it is rarely expressed in such terms, stage hypnotism is actually a sales situation. Your whole approach is to routine the show so that each successive test *sells* the subject on responding to the next; thus each test is important to the success of the one that follows, forming a chain reaction that flows through the entire show. *For this reason, routine your show so that the beginning simple experiments lead up gradually towards the more complex.* Properly routined, "progressive selling" is a major secret in the success of the hypnotic show.

The High Pressure of Stage Hypnotism

If ever the term, "high pressure selling" were applicable, it is in describing the techniques of the stage hypnotist. Every psychological device the performer can muster is thrown in a continuous barrage at the subjects to produce the proper mental conditions for hypnosis. The "high pressure" must be artfully handled however, for to be effective as a technique it must be subtle.

Repetition and Clearness of Suggestions

In order for the mind in the hypnotic state to properly assimilate and react to suggestions they must be understood, and to that end be clearly given. Accordingly, it is often well to repeat your suggestive ideas. In my practice, I usually repeat every suggestion at least two times in order that it may be properly assimilated by the subject, and secondly I make a special effort to speak clearly, simply, and directly to the subject, or subjects as the case may be.

One Thing at a Time

Always remember this basic rule in the giving of hypnotic suggestions: *only present one idea or suggestion series at a time, and after the response to the suggestions has occurred, remove the influence completely before further ideas are presented.* This is very important not only to your personal success in hypnotizing but to your subjects' well being as well.

Don't Expect Too Much

In presenting suggestions to your subjects, don't offer them ideas which are too foreign to their natures. Gauge the tests you try with each subject within his capacity. If you will keep in mind this rule, your work will prove far more striking in the production of effective hypnotic phenomena.

Use Your Best Subjects

Here is a secret always to be applied. As your act progresses, you can invariably spot your most responsive subjects. *Now use these good subjects for your more critical, individual tests.* They thus function as responsive leaders that set examples for the other subjects in the committee to follow.

Trance Depth in Stage Demonstrations

This is a psychological question, of course. Although it will naturally vary with different invididuals, in general the depth of trance produced via the rapid techniques of stage hypnotism will not be as deep as that developed by slower, more methodical methods when opportunity permits of longer induction procedures. This makes little difference to the practical performer other than that such must be taken in consideration in the handling of his subjects. *To this end, make it your rule to plan your stage hypnotism tests of a type that are easy for your subjects to perform.*

From the audience's point-of-view, lighter trance hypnotic experiments are as effective as more advanced demonstrations. So, until you are certain of your respective subject's trance depth don't expect too much of him or her, and guage your inital stage experiments to lighter hypnosis levels.

Keeping the Subjects Entranced

The stage methods of hypnotizing are so rapid and performed in mass that they tend to be somewhat unstable, so unless pressure is maintained to carry the subjects along, some persons are apt to slip spontaneously out of hypnosis if left too long by themselves. *To avoid this, it is a good rule to keep your subjects active and busy responding to various suggestions; then awaken them between tests rather than just leaving them sleeping in hypnosis unattended.*

It is important also, to give sleep retaining suggestions at intervals, such as, "Nothing will disturb or awaken you until I tell you to awaken. You are going down deeper and deeper to sleep in hypnosis continuously with every breath you take. Nothing will disturb you." Such suggestions tend to overcome the tendency of stage subject to awaken of their own accord.

Simulation

Some subjects, in the stage situation, tend to simulate hypnosis rather than actually going completely into the trance state. This simulation is not necessarily voluntary deception, for it is frequently born of a sincere desire to cooperate with the performer and assist in the show, yet not possessing the innate mental makeup for achieving real somnambulism such a subject does his very best to imitate the genuine condition.

While it is not necessary to dismiss subjects who are simulating hypnosis, as they are striving to cooperate and often subsequently slip into genuine trance, it is well that you be able to spot them so they are not featured in special tests. Leave such subjects in the background, bringing the real subjects forwards so the audience can see authentic phenomena throughout your show.

Deliberate Faking

It is a far cry from the simulating subject who is trying his best for the success of the show to the subject who deliberately pretends to be hypnotized just to fool you. *This latter subject is dangerous to your prestige as a hypnotist.* Such subjects have a way of pretending to be asleep while you are watching them, and when your back is turned open their eyes and poke fun at you, and them seemingly return to sleep before you can spot them.

So keep a wary eye out for such pranksters as they can greatly harm your show. Sometimes they are quite clever and are difficult to catch, but if you are on your guard you will shortly discover the offender. One way is to keep your ears pealed for laughs, and whenever a laugh from the audience comes for no apparent reason, be alerted to the possibility that someone is faking, and spot the trouble-maker as soon as possible, and once you do locate him dismiss him from the stage immediately. Be firm and insistent about the matter. You will find that the audience will applaud you for thus disposing of a distrubing influence.

Another way to catch these fakes is to occasionally unexpectedly turn around, or have someone stationed in the wings who watches the subjects constantly, and if he sees that a subject is faking, hold up the number of his fingers which represents the chair number in which the offending subject is seated.

It is in the attention to details that the mediocre becomes great, so, too, is it with hypnotism.

On Judging Subjects

The question of who to dismiss and who to retain on stage is important to the success of the hypnotism show. The hypnotist must become an expert at this selection.

As an audience participation show composed of volunteers, the performer becomes, in a sense, "the game master," as they term such in England. He must learn how to dismiss, retain, use, and place his players to the best advantage for the success of his show and the entertainment of his audience. The more proficient he can become at assumming this role the more successful a hypnotic showman he will be. It calls for knowledge and diplomancy.

Dismissing subjects from the stage takes tact, and there are times when it is not well to dismiss anyone, as, for example, when the volunteers are few in numbers or have been difficult to secure from the audience. All persons who volunteer should be given a chance to prove their hypnotic worth, and only subjects who are obviously detrimental to the show should be dismissed. If any dismissals are to be made, such should be done during the first one-thrid of the show, which allows a full two-thrids of the show for working with superior hypnotics in the advanced experiments.

In the event of an overwhelming crowd of volunteers coming on stage, a mass waking suggestion test, such as "Hand Locking," can be given the stage full of people at the very beginning of the show, and then retain all those who succeed in the test and dismiss all those who do not. This is diplomatic handling and automatically selects out of the crowd of people those who are the best subjects and eliminates the others. You can then seat those who remain on stage and start the show.

Add to Public Knowledge the Value of the Therapeutic Side of Hypnotism

The real value of the science and practice of hypnotism lies not in the fields of the entertainer but in the fields of therapy. Important research and healings are being accomplished through its proper use by medical men and certified psychologists. Dentists, too, have found it useful in their practices. The public should know of these things, the quality of his performing can become a most useful public relations man for the art/science of hypnotism.

Study the Literature On Hypnotism Etc.

With the scope of the knowledge that lies before you it is little wonder that the success of the hypnotism show becomes a certainity, and that the marvels of hypnotic entertainment leave audiences gasping. These are your secrets to be used to make entertaining with hypnotism a true art.

The field of hypnotism is vast, and the scope and possibilities of developing the hypnotism show great. It can be staged as simply as an informal lecture or as pretentiously as a theatrical production.

With the information you have at your fingertips of how to hypnotize, present, routine, and stage the hypnotism show, nothing remains but to apply with skill that knowledge.

As an additional word of advise, I cannot do better than recommend that you steep yourself in hypnotic literature. *Read everything about hypnosis you can get your hands on.* A visit to the library will reward you with many titles. Study the old classics along with contemporary books on the subjects. The accompanying bibliography in this book suggests many worthwhile titles for your further study.

In your study of hypnotism, you will find various conflicts in theory and practice as presented by different authors. However, to you as an entertaining hypnotist such makes little difference. It all forms basic knowledge, and with the assimilation of that knowledge *hypnotism will become second nature to you.* It is then that you really become a hypnotist. So talk it, read it, study it, and above all practice it.

As the famous illusionist, Howard Thurston once advised in regard to mastering the art of magic, "If you want to be a successful magician, three things are essential -- practice, practice, and more practice." Such applies with equal force to hypnotism.

From forty years of experience as a professional stage hypnotist, I know of no better way of judging in advance how successful the show is going to be than the fact that if the volunteers flock onto the stage, when you invite the committee up, you can count on it being a successful show! *An eager group of volunteers -- that want to be hypnotized -- is your guarantee to a wonderful performance.* Conversely, if the subjects are loth to come forward and have to be coaxed up, and you have difficulty filling the chairs, then you can count on it being a difficult show. When the conditions are right you will find the hypnotism show will flow along easily; when the conditions are not right it will prove just the opposite; it is then that you must be a professional.

For entertaining with hypnotism, let me go on record as stating that your entire success will be summed up in the one word, FAITH. Faith in yourself compelling the faith of your subject(s) and your audience(s) in the law of the great hypnotist. Of such is the art of professional stage hypnotism which provides an opportunity to exhibit some of the most remarkable phenomena in the world.

22
After the Hypnotism Show

Your will find your hypnotism show will continue on backstage after the entertainment is over. Many people will flock around to see you, often asking you to hypnotize them privately.

Such requests as wanting to stop smoking, overcoming drinking and overeating, correcting fingernail biting, and mastering various psychological difficulties such as stuttering, etc are common.

The stage hypnotist should appreciate that he is an entertainer not a therapist and steer clear from all such requests by flatly refusing to perform any applications of hypnotherapy. There are two reasons for this: the first is purely personal in that such work is extremely time consuming, and the one session possible in after-the-show situations is of little value to the patient anyway. Such inflictions are usually based on some underlying psychological reason that has to be first sought out by an expert before a permanent cure can be affected. And secondly, therapy is not his field, such belongs in the hands of qualified medical men and psychologists. In other words, therapy should be left in the hands of the professional hypnotherapist just as hypnotic entertainment should be in the hands of the professional stage hypnotist.

As a stage hypnotist, you can handle all such matters diplomatically simply by stating that your work is entirely that of an entertainer, and for such therapeutic applications a doctor should be consulted who can advise correctly on the matter.

DVD's of Ormond McGill

STAGE HYPNOSIS
PART ONE: GIL BOYNE – From 1960 to 1965, Gil Boyne entertained thousands with his "Hilarious Hypnosis" Stage Show in nightclubs throughout the USA This video tape combines one full hour of highly-skilled stage hypnosis techniques with the hilarious antics of a stage full of subjects.
PART TWO: ORMOND MCGILL -- Ormond McGill, Dean of American Hypnotists, presents a fascinating and mirth provoking one-hour show in his unique style. This is your opportunity to compare and learn from the art of two of the world's great stage hypnotists.

INTUITIVE HYPNOTHERAPY
ORMOND MCGILL AND MARLEEN MULDER
Ormond and Marleen present Intuitive Hypnotherapy as a path for therapist and client to discover practical and spiritual insight and choices to enhance the art of living.

ORIENTAL METHODS OF HYPNOTIZING
ORMOND MCGILL
Based on his extensive travels in India, Ormond demonstrates the Oriental Method of Hypnotizing as you learn the power of visualization, affirmation and projection.

FOR A COMPLETE LIST OF HYPNOTISM, HYPNOTHERAPY AND MIND POWER BOOKS, CD's AND DVD's SEE
http://www.westwoodpublishingco.com